Human Rights:
Changing the Culture

T0366884

Edited by

Luke Clements
and
James Young

ISBN 0–631–21755–X

First Published 1999

Published simultaneously as Vol. 26 No. 1 of
Journal of Law and Society ISSN 0263–323X

Blackwell Publishers
108 Cowley Road, Oxford OX4 1JF, UK
and
350 Main Street, Malden, MA 02148, USA.

British Library Cataloguing in Publication Data applied for

Library of Congress Cataloguing-in-Publication Data applied for

Printed on acid free recycled paper

Contents

JOURNAL OF LAW AND SOCIETY
VOLUME 26, NUMBER 1, MARCH 1999
ISSN: 0263-323X, pp. 1-5

Human Rights: Changing the Culture

LUKE CLEMENTS* AND JAMES YOUNG*

The Human Rights Act 1998 is likely to come into force early year next year. It unquestionably has the potential for being one of the most fundamental constitutional enactments since the Bill of Rights over 300 years ago. While so much constitutional change in the United Kingdom has been achieved without resort to legislation, this is a deliberate part of a programme of constitutional change by legislation.[1] The legislation has to be seen in the context of the government's wider programme of constitutional reform: the reform of the House of Lords, the promised Freedom of Information Act, devolution to Scotland, Wales, and Northern Ireland, and elected mayors. Any evaluation of a change in the way in which the constitution is perceived and imagined in the United Kingdom cannot ignore the interrelationship of these reforms. The scope of this collection of essays is, however, narrower. It is to consider what changes have brought about this particular constitutional reform and its potential for creating a 'human rights culture'.

THE EUROPEAN CONVENTION ON HUMAN RIGHTS

The Act 'incorporates' the European Convention on Human Rights and Fundamental Freedoms into the laws of the United Kingdom. The United Kingdom has been a party to this Convention since it entered into force in 1953, but only accepted the right of an individual to petition to the European Commission of Human Rights[2] complaining of a breach of the Convention in 1966, when it accepted the compulsory jurisdiction of the European Court of Human Rights. The background to the Convention is briefly discussed in the essay by James Young, but it may help readers, especially non-European ones, to understand some of the arguments if the structure of the Convention is briefly sketched.

1 Labour Party, *Manifesto* (1997).
2 This body has ceased to exist and been replaced by a restructured European Court of Human Rights since 1 November 1998.

* Cardiff Law School, P.O Box 427, Museum Avenue, Cardiff CF1 1XD, Wales

1

The main body of the Convention outlines the main traditional political and civil rights: right to life, freedom from torture and inhuman or degrading treatment, freedom from slavery or forced labour, freedom of the person, right to a fair trial, prohibition on retrospective criminal legislation, right to privacy, freedom of conscience, freedom of expression, freedom of assembly, the right to marry. All these rights are to be secured without discrimination on grounds of 'sex, race, colour, language, religion, political or other opinion, national or social origin, association with a national minority property, birth or other status'. What differentiates the Convention from most national Bills of Rights is the way in which the Convention seeks to elaborate the circumstances in which the state may restrict and interfere with the protected rights. To take as an illustration the right of privacy in Article 8:[3]

> There shall be no interference by a public authority with the exercise of this right except such as is in accordance with the law and is necessary in a democratic society in the interests of national security, public safety or the economic well-being of the country, for the prevention of disorder or crime, for the protection of health or morals, or for the protection of the rights and freedoms of others.

In other words, the Convention places at the forefront of the readers' mind that all rights are limited and may be subject to restriction. This is, of course, accepted in all countries which profess to protect human rights, but this is generally either implicitly understood, as in the Constitution of the United States of America, or made the subject of a general clause, reminding users that rights are not absolute and may be subject to certain limits.[4]

THE HUMAN RIGHTS ACT

The Act reworks the historic compromise inherent in the turbulent relations between Parliament, the executive, and the judiciary without at first sight creating uncontrollable new vortices. Parliament remains supreme but the executive will be obliged on occasions to satisfy the High Court that a particular law is 'just' in the sense that it does not contravene the European Convention on Human Rights. If the Court is not satisfied, then it can say so, by declaring the law 'incompatible' with the Convention; it cannot however strike down primary legislation. The Act makes provision for what occurs in such cases; essentially, a declaration of incompatibility will trigger Parliamentary action leading to statutory amendment.

The Convention, once incorporated, will place respect for human rights at the centre of any legal dispute. To this extent it is, as Luke Clements

---

3 'Everyone has the right to respect for his private and family life, his home and his correspondence.'

4 '. . . the rights and freedoms contained in this Bill of Rights may be subject only to such reasonable limits prescribed by law as can be demonstrably justified in a free and democratic society' – the identical wording of section 1 of the Canadian Charter of Rights and Freedoms 1982 and the New Zealand Bill of Rights Act, section 5.

2

argues in his paper, new and radical equity; as equity trumped the common law, Convention submissions will now take precedence and render even primary statutes vulnerable to summary revision. Section 3 of the Act obliges all courts to interpret legislation so as to uphold the Convention rights and this rule of construction will apply to past as well as future legislation. The higher Courts will therefore be required to revisit and possibly reverse their previous decisions; in the next few years we are likely in consequence to see a significant erosion of the principle of judicial precedent The Act makes it unlawful for public authorities to act in a way which is incompatible with the Convention and anyone who is materially affected by such an unlawful act will be able to bring proceedings against the authority including a claim for damages.

The Act is however primarily a constitutional creature, preoccupied with the legitimacy of the United Kingdom's democratic label. The executive is too powerful in Westminster and the only realistic compensation for the relative weakness of Parliament is the enhanced role for the judiciary provided for by the Human Rights Act. Whatever legitimacy local politicians have, it is increasingly difficult to argue that it is a democratic one when almost three-quarters of the population do not vote in local elections. Again, the right of individuals or minority groups to challenge the 'justice and proportionality' of a local government decision goes a long way to restoring constitutional legitimacy (if not the democratic label). To this extent therefore the Act can be seen as a legitimate strand to the modernizing, reforming movement of local government, reform which encompasses best value, the issue of social exclusion, the obligation to promote economic and social well-being and, in time, electoral reform. As Luke Clements points out, incorporation of the European Convention on Human Rights also has the advantage of adding intellectual weight to a reform agenda that at times has been seen as lacking philosophical *gravitas*.

A NEW CULTURE OF RIGHTS

In compiling this collection, we have endeavoured to bring together articles which adopt a common theme and yet consider widely differing segments of the socio-legal spectrum. The pervasive theme is the Act's likely impact on the United Kingdom's legal culture. Human rights provisions are now the norm in national constitutions. After the Second World War, Germany and Italy acquired constitutions with strong human rights provision. So did European countries in the Soviet block. These 'socialist' constitutions were a mockery, since the gap between law and practice was wider than the most cynical western commentator might find in their chosen jurisdiction. Yet after 1989 and the collapse of communism in Europe, the newly independent democratic states rushed towards constitutional Bills of Rights.

The idea of creating a human rights culture or a culture of rights has been a recurrent theme in political debates surrounding the Human Rights Act.

3

The increased volume of cases in which lawyers and judges take the Convention into account suggests that already a new way of thinking is developing. Indeed, as James Young suggests, this is one of the reasons that the Human Rights Act has been relatively uncontroversial. Although the government has refrained from spelling out precisely what a rights culture involves, Murray Hunt suggests that it is certainly more communitarian or 'social-democratic' than libertarian. Tom Campbell questions the democratic legitimacy of judicially enforced rights. He also emphasizes how the Act falls short of a United States-style Bill of Rights. For him the Act appears as a modest step, in which judicial power may be contained within the democratic process. The perceived balance between executive, legislature, and judiciary may indicate this, and it is his contention that it leaves room for a culture of controversy: one in which the concretization of rights must be recognized as contested and contestable and not simply positive law interpreted and applied by the courts. It remains to be seen whether this is how this relationship will develop in practice.

Two papers provide an international perspective. The Netherlands and Canada are both countries which have adopted enforceable human rights legislation as mature democracies. Bert Swart and John Hucker explore the impact of human rights instruments upon their domestic legal cultures. Swart, concentrating on criminal procedure, demonstrates the way in which the Convention has transformed rules of law and judicial thinking. His focus on Article 6 of the Convention and criminal procedure demonstrates the radical changes which may be effected when the underlying philosophy of a Convention provision is significantly at odds with the assumptions underlying domestic law. Significantly, the confrontation of domestic law and the Convention has led to change which would have been unlikely if the interpretation of the Convention had been left in the hand of the Dutch courts. Criminal procedure may not be the primary battleground in the United Kingdom, but there will be such areas of conflict. The English common law (or absence of law) of privacy is certainly an area ripe for litigation.

Much has been made of the Canadian Charter of Rights and Freedoms and the influence of United States constitutional practice. John Hucker takes us away from litigation in the Canadian Supreme Court and reveals in his paper some of the significant pitfalls that may lie ahead. By considering in some detail three quite different issues which have arisen in Canada, he highlights the difficulties that tribunals have encountered when trying to adjudicate upon disputes which do not fall neatly under the head of abuse of state power. In his opinion, the Court's procrustean approach to civil and political rights has caused it to be far from sure-footed when dealing with issues which, on inspection, raise significant socio-economic or minority rights questions. This finds an echo in Tom Campbell's concern about the dangers of the judiciary straying onto this slippery slope. He questions whether it is even possible in the sphere of political and civil rights, to concretize our understanding of those rights to the level of specificity

4

required to determine specific cases. His misgivings about the juridification of politics reflects views long held by the left political élite and experienced in Canada. It also finds an echo in Murray Hunt's concern as to whether a conservative legal profession will break out of its habits of thought. As James Young illustrates, the fear of taking rights out of the hands of the politicians and placing them in the hands of judges has long been a subject of unease in the United Kingdom debate. Without the pervasive influence of Europe and the stridency of Thatcherism, the judiciary might not have been won over in the United Kingdom in the way he describes.

On a United Kingdom level, Murray Hunt develops the theme of harmonizing the incorporation of the Convention with the new constitutional order that this government seeks to bring about. He analyses (from the perspective of a practising barrister) the degree to which the prevailing legal culture will be able to resist the government's attempt to shift that very culture into a new honesty about the role of lawyers in law-making and towards a new readiness to advocate human rights norms when adjudicating upon difficult and controversial question of public morality. He questions whether the judiciary will be able to discard their private law focus which obscures the wider issues which are often at stake in human rights litigation.

The impact of the new Act upon a specific legal area, and the wider political lessons to be drawn from this are considered by Philip Fennell. His paper examines the specific field of mental health law, an area which already bears the indelible stamp of Strasbourg jurisprudence. The Mental Health Act 1983 is in large part a response to the judgments of the European Court of Human Rights twenty years ago. He shows how the simplistic 'negative rights' approach to the Convention, characteristically the approach of the common law, fails in relation to the rights of mentally disordered patients, and how the Strasbourg Court has developed the 'positive rights' elements inherent within Article 5. The new legalism that emerges from this developing jurisprudence has, he concludes, much in common with the present government's 'third way'.

The Human Rights Act is part of a new constitutional settlement. Expectations range from the unrealistically optimistic to the pessimistically cynical. We do not align ourselves with either of these views, nor do any of the papers in this collection. From Tom Campbell's reflections on the philosophical problems of positivizing human rights to Luke Clements's radical suspicions of the desire of the state to enfeeble the effects of its own reforms, all the authors identify the philosophical and practical dilemmas which face politicians, lawyers, campaigners, and the victims of the power of the state or of the failure of the state to protect the powerless from the powerful. It may be doubtful whether a rights culture equivalent to that in the United States of America will develop in the United Kingdom, or whether the Human Rights Act, the creature of a legal élite, will remain the property of that élite. There is, however, no doubt that public law discourse will never be the same again.

5

JOURNAL OF LAW AND SOCIETY
VOLUME 26, NUMBER 1, MARCH 1999
ISSN: 0263–323X, pp. 6–26

Human Rights: A Culture of Controversy

TOM CAMPBELL*

*Many arguments in favour of constitutionally entrenched Bills of Rights
are undermined by the inherently controversial nature of human rights
with respect to their content, their form, and their valence. Even in the
case of civil and political rights, the concretization of rights at the level
of specificity required to decide particular cases must always be politically
and morally controversial. There is no accepted moral or legal method
that can be utilized to give the requisite objectivity to the value choices
inherent in human rights jurisprudence. Positivization of human rights
increases their utility but compromises their moral status. It follows
that legitimate articulation of human rights requires ongoing democratic
dialogue and decision-making. Although perceived as a stop-gap measure,
the Human Rights Act 1998 could facilitate an enduring partnership
between courts and parliaments, placing human rights more firmly on the
political agenda and establishing a proper balance between the inputs of
courts and parliaments which recognizes that the development of positivized human rights must be primarily located in electorally-based politics.*

The Human Rights Act may turn out to be a minor or a major change in
the constitution of the United Kingdom but, either way, it has to be viewed
as part of a global trend towards the legal institutionalization of the idea of
human rights. This can only be welcomed if it places the identification and
protection of fundamental human interests nearer the centre of the public
agenda, but the entrenchment of court-based determinations of the content
and form to be given to the concept of basic rights is a potentially dangerous
development to the extent that it leads to the juridification of politics and
the distancing of the prioritization and concretization of human rights from
the domain of representative politics. Human rights will be the weaker if
they are seen as the impositions of controversial interpretations of basic
rights outwith the scope of democratic accountability.

* *Professor of Law, Faculty of Law, The Australian National University,
ACT 0200, Australia*

The alternatives facing the United Kingdom with respect to the European Convention on Human Rights (ECHR) are quite restricted in the context of its membership of the European Union. Some constitutional changes are clearly required to remove the anomalies arising from British courts being unable to take significant cognizance of the ECHR even although its citizens may challenge their decisions at the European Court of Human Rights. The Human Rights Act appears to be at the modest end of the range of alternatives, but it may be no more than a staging post to a fully-fledged domestic Bill of Rights, in which case there will be a difficult debate on which specific rights and what mode of entrenchment are to be adopted. In fact, the emergence of a so-called home-grown Bill of Rights seems an increasingly unlikely outcome as the problems of drawing up such a Bill become more apparent. If a stop-gap Human Rights Act turns out to be a more permanent feature of the British constitution, the ECHR may continue to have relatively slight impact on British courts, but its import will depend largely on the way that British judiciaries respond to the opportunities which it creates for more activist judicial roles. There is a possibility that the Act could encourage judicial creativity not only in statutory interpretation but also in the development of the common law in line with European Human Rights jurisprudence.

Whatever the outcome of the current constitutional fluidity, it is timely to reflect on the choice of mechanisms available to a country with a strong tradition of parliamentary democracy in adapting to an existing regional human rights system. This involves examining the shifting lines of debate about the nature and function of human rights and revisiting some of the familiar philosophical problems which dog the human rights movement by casting doubt on the epistemology of human rights. The principal point deriving from this reflection is that no institutional mechanisms which neglect the existence of radical and reasonable controversy as to the content, form, and valence of basic rights can be justified. A cognate suggestion is that there are aspects of the Human Rights Act which may serve to promote fruitful political dialogue between courts as primarily monitors and parliaments as the primary legislators of human rights, a partnership which permits the development of human rights law to reflect a fuller range of interests than the ECHR currently encompasses. If the use made of the new judicial powers is temperate and sensitive to the wider democratic context, it may turn out that there are good reasons for accepting something like the current Act as a working compromise between legal and the political inputs to the articulation of human rights law.

❦

HUMAN RIGHTS CONTROVERSIES

Although the nature and significance of human rights has been debated for so long and in so many spheres, the lines of disagreement on the best way to conceive and institutionalize human rights are still far from clear. We may view the shifting areas of engagement in the dimensions of constitutional law, philosophical scrutiny, and ideological compromise.[1]

In the constitutional debate we have passed the stage where it is simply assumed that to be supportive of the human rights movement it is necessary to advocate a United States-style constitution with an entrenched Bill of Rights and a judicial override of legislative enactments. There is at least the beginnings of a debate within the human rights fold as to the best method for the identification, articulation, and enforcement of human rights, particularly amongst those who give particular weight to the right of political self-determination.[2] Although it is widely assumed that, in recent times, courts have tended to make more progressive decisions than legislatures on human rights, this has not always been the case and is far from guaranteed in the future.[3] It is also frequently acknowledged that changing the role of courts can have far-reaching and predictable effects on the nature of judicial appointments and on the conduct of those appointed to 'interpret' superficially attractive but worryingly vague statements of principle. History amply demonstrates that courts can thwart as well as facilitate progressive social, political, and economic changes. Indeed, it may be that those who turn in disillusionment from politicians to judges may find that the latter can offer little protection against the resurgences of regressive political movements which are more likely to emerge when we reduce our expectations of representative politics with respect to the furtherance and defence of fundamental civil, political, social, cultural, and economic rights.

Nevertheless, while it is no longer axiomatic amongst supporters of human rights reform that such rights are best sustained through court-administered Bills of Rights, there is still an unjustifiably high burden of proof placed on those who are worried by the long-term constitutional consequences of making the progressive delineation of individual rights primarily the responsibility of courts by enacting constitutional changes which, it is generally agreed, transfer very significant political powers to courts, either within or outwith the boundaries of the state. Such far-reaching constitutional development may seem attractive, especially at a time when politics and politicians are held in such low regard, but their eventual impact on how citizens go about settling their political differences may well be seriously detrimental to electoral politics and thus to the legitimacy of governments. Further, it needs to be acknowledged that changes which entrench judicial power are harder to reverse than they are to implement. There is, therefore, reason to examine very carefully alternative ways of enunciating, protecting, and furthering basic human interests.

1 Much of the background theory for this essay draws on T. Campbell, *The Left and Rights: A Conceptual Analysis of the Idea of Socialist Rights* (1983).
2 Thus, C. Nino, *The Constitution of Deliberative Democracy* (1993) and J.Waldron, 'A Rights-Based Critique of Constitutional Rights' (1993) 13 *Oxford J. of Legal Studies* 18.
3 For instance, see D. Tucker, 'Natural Law or Common Law: Human Rights in Australia' in *Rethinking Human Rights*, eds. B. Galligan and C. Sampford (1997) 120–43.

8

In the philosophical debate we have passed the stage where human rights are automatically associated with natural law and held to be incompatible with adherence to legal positivism.[4] Supporters of human rights do not now generally endorse a naturalistic moral epistemology whereby the content of human rights is read off from the essence of human nature or some religious view thereof. Many legal positivists welcome the use of human rights rhetoric to identify core societal goals and have no problems either with the institutionalization of specified rights and duties as lexically prior to any conflicting legislation or with such rights and duties being given a special status within a democratic system of governance. Indeed, it is possible to see the progressive institutionalization of human rights through the development by human rights courts of juristic doctrines and case law as a positivization of purely moral rights whereby intangible generalized values are given specific content. The human rights rules thus concretized by the courts gain authority from a newly identified social source of law. In identifying a social origin for human rights law, these developments may be seen as compatible with the 'sources thesis' that is commonly taken to define the theory of legal positivism.[5] On the other hand, the often nebulous content of human rights prescriptions comes up against the problems which such highly indeterminate legal norms present to a positivist ideal of the rule of law as an impartially administered system of clear, precise, and determinate rules. In general, a positivist approach to human rights has the advantage of encouraging the creation of specific rules capable of guiding state conduct and providing bases for predictable remedies for violations of human rights without claiming that these can be deduced from self-evident or uncontroversial premises.

However, although legal positivists may welcome the moves to concretize or positivize human rights by rendering them more specific and justiciable,[6] this same process may also be seen as a way of weakening the capacity of courts to develop human rights law in accordance with enduring or emerging moral ideals.[7] The development of case law snares human rights in the tangled web of precedent and legal authority, thus threatening to devitalize its moral force in a way which is historically exemplified by the progressive positivization of equity. There is therefore a powerful body of opinion in favour of having human rights law expressed only in the form of vague prescriptions which invite moral deliberation and textually unfettered discretionary decision-making by human rights courts without a major prior commitment to existing case law. From this point of view, to resist the creation of the massive judicial power inherent in such a discretionary model

---

4 For further analysis, see T. Campbell, *The Legal Theory of Ethical Positivism* (1996) 161–87.
5 J. Raz, *The Authority of Law* (1979) 47 ff.
6 For examples, see T. Campbell et al. (eds.), *Human Rights: from Rhetoric to Reality* (1986).
7 As in R. Wasserstrom, 'Rights, Human Rights and Racial Discrimination' (1964) 61 *J. of Philosophy* 630. See, also, J. Feinberg, 'The Nature and Value of Rights' (1970) 4 *J. of Value Enquiry* 243.

is taken to be a rejection of human rights *per se* rather than an attempt to uphold the rule of law through distinguishing the power to formulate rules from the duty to apply them.

Such a system of moral supervision is defensible, however, only to the extent that there is accessible knowledge of objective universal values available to courts. It may be seen as an achievement of the human rights movement that there is a widespread belief that such knowledge is indeed available. However, as we will see, this neo-natural law philosophy with its high confidence in the accessibility of human rights to human reason and the capacity of judges to reach an objective assessment of the content and priority of such rights far outstrips any available epistemological foundations which would justify taking such issues outside the domain of political disagreement.

In the ideological debate, we have passed the stage when human rights are associated primarily with a form of extreme libertarianism, wherein the essential purpose of human rights is to corral the activities of government into a highly constricted domain in order that individuals, either alone or in free association, may pursue their own good in their own way. While some demands for court-articulated human rights do stem from the ideal of minimal government whereby the egalitarian welfare policies sometimes favoured by popular majorities are seen as endangering fundamental rights and freedoms, it is now widely recognized that state activity is often required to realize many of the priority interests of all human beings and that these interests have as much right to be upheld as fundamental rights as the negative liberties of the traditional liberal state.[8]

It is true that the division between civil and political rights, on the one hand, and economic, social, and cultural rights, on the other, remains politically salient. This division is marked at the international level in the different status of the International Covenant on Civil and Political Rights and the International Covenant on Economic, Social and Cultural Rights and at the European level in the distinction between the European Convention of Human Rights and the European Social Charter, which represent the continuing tendencies to regard civil liberties as intrinsically more basic than material needs and to assume that the prime role of the human rights movement is to limit the evil that governments do rather than encourage governments to become more pro-active in the cause of fundamental human interests. Nevertheless, we may note the formal commitment of the United Nations to the equal importance of both types of rights[9] and the repeated attempts to demonstrate that there is no hard and fast distinction between costless civil and political rights and expensive economic and social rights

---

8 Thus, C. Fabre, 'Constitutionalising Social Rights' (1998) 6 *J. of Political Philosophy* 263, 283: 'if one advocates constitutional civil and political rights as well as social rights, then one must advocate *constitutional* social rights'.

9 Vienna Declaration and Program of Action (1993) 14 *Human Rights Law J.* 352.

10

which could justify the mandatory status of the former and the purely aspirational status of the latter.[10]

Moreover, current human rights regimes are beginning to have a dated look in that their emphasis remains on the sins of government rather than the evils of capitalism, if we may still use that term to identify the contemporary forms of private economic power. There is nothing in the concept, as distinct from the history, of human rights which requires us to identify states as the prime violators of such rights, and there is a serious incompleteness in an ideology which purports to identify and protect basic human interests while failing to address the suffering which is perpetrated by increasingly globalized private economic power. This is not to say that human rights are incompatible with capitalism any more than they are incompatible with government. Rather, it is to assert that economic power has the same systematic ambivalence for human good and ill as does political power.

There is a tendency to assume that the demise of Soviet-style communism represents a triumph of the way in which human rights have evolved within the jurisdictions of the cold war victors. The globalization of liberalism is often portrayed as the globalization of libertarianism. However, freeing up the association of human rights with libertarianism or negative liberalism has been assisted rather than retarded by the dissolution of the cold war which has increased the prospect of new ideological configurations. The specifics of human rights no longer need to be drawn with an eye to their role in an ideological battle between capitalism and communism.

In this debate, the ideological implications of rights discourse is distorted by those who consider rights to be incompatible with life in a caring community of persons whose conduct is characterized by a degree of altruism and goodwill to others. This critique develops from Marx's scathing denunciation of inalienable rights as bourgeois ideology and is now common in communitarian and feminist writing.[11] These sceptical views of rights have much historical justification but miss the point, which is crucial for assessing the potential of rights, that the interests which are identified and protected by rights need not be construed in terms of narrow self-interest, but can include interests which caring persons have in assisting and supporting other people, interests which have a strong claim to be fundamental in a society of social beings.[12]

Moreover, the fact that citizens have rights does not require that they exercise these rights purely in their own interest. Indeed, it does not require that they exercise their rights as a matter of course, since, in the great majority of cases, having a right includes the right to waive that right.[13] Critical discussions of the culture of rights too readily assume that the culture of rights is the culture of individual egotism, which encourages and promotes

10 H. Steiner and P. Alston (eds.), *International Human Rights in Context* (1996) 256–328.
11 For a balanced view of the latter debate, see E. Kingdom, *What's Wrong with Rights* (1991).
12 Campbell, op. cit., n. 1, p. 83.
13 M.J. Meyer, 'When Not to Claim your Rights: The Abuse and the Virtuous Use of Rights' (1997) 5 *J. of Political Philosophy* 14.

11

people to assert their own interests in conflict with those of others. It is possible to conceive of a system of rights as a framework of rules that can be drawn upon to promote fundamental human interests without a culture in which the citizens seek only their own self-advancement. Rights may be instrumental for a variety of purposes, including the capacity to confer benefits on others within a culture which includes a role for autonomous judgement by morally good people as to how and when they exercise their rights. A culture of rights need not be a culture of complaint.

There is another fascinating coincidence of seemingly incompatible trends in current political ideology in the acceptance of political globalization in the form of democratic systems on the American model in conjunction with the affirmation of the neglected significance of cultural diversity. The circle is squared formally by affirming the universal significance of cultural diversity and materially by requiring that a democratic system ought not to permit rules or practices which discriminate on certain unacceptable grounds, such as race, ethnicity, national origins or gender. This leaves unresolved what to do with those cultural differences which embody incompatible positions on such matters as basic criminal law, the role of religious authority or the political legitimacy of different forms of government. Nor does it enable us to deal with conflicting views of what are and what are not acceptable grounds for differential treatment. It also leaves unresolved the tension between the idea of protecting individual members of a cultural group from unacceptable discrimination in the wider society and the idea of promoting the distinctiveness of cultures which encourage precisely such discriminations within their own groups.

In summary, it remains true to say that it is often assumed that to be opposed to allocating power over the definition of human rights to courts is tantamount to being hostile to human rights as such, despite the significance and implications of the basic right to self-determination underlying all democratic theory. It is also assumed that human rights are and must remain primarily moral or natural rights in that courts must use their moral judgements or knowledge of natural law to determine which legislative enactments are permitted. This goes with the further assumption that human rights can be based on some objectivist morality whereby, through religious authority, moral intuition or natural science, a society, or identified segments of it, can, by adopting the proper epistemology of morals, be trusted to come up with the 'correct' reading and import of such matters as 'the right to life' or 'the right to food'. In this context, there are still those who equate relativism, the thesis that what is good and right for one group may not be good and right for another group, with subjectivism, the thesis that the epistemology of moral judgement privileges individual preferences thus undermining the moral universalism on which human rights are based. Finally, it is also often assumed that a devotion to human rights is a commitment to some version of libertarianism whereby the interests of the non-responsible individual are paramount within the political system.

12

All these assumptions can be challenged, and need to be debated if we are to think clearly about how the future of human rights is best secured and which constitutional and cultural directions to take if we wish to promote our preferred versions of the content, form, and force of such rights as we believe we ought to have. In making such challenges and furthering such debate, we must take note of the contestability of almost every aspect of human rights and look for ways of institutionalizing human rights which retain primary political control over determining the content, form, and valence of human rights within representative politics, and do so in a manner which recognizes the inherently controversial nature of the specification of such rights, leaving scope for the further assimilation of social and economic rights and permitting a measure of cultural diversity within the domain of human rights.

THE EPISTEMOLOGY OF HUMAN RIGHTS

The philosophical problems for human rights centre on the lack of a clear method for identifying the content of such rights and the associated phenomenon of ideological capture, whereby the all-important details of human rights are filled out in an evaluatively partisan way. Problematic also are the confusions arising from the existence of different conceptions of the form of rights and their correlative obligations, if any, with respect to their nature (for example, negative or positive) or their status (for example, moral or legal), matters which have significant political consequences.

It is difficult to grapple with these epistemological issues without adopting a position with respect to the ontology of human rights, the issue as to whether rights have some sort of independent and objective existence, as part, perhaps, of some socially pre-existent natural law, or whether they are entirely creatures of human creativity to be moulded and developed to human designs without the restrictions of a metaphysical reality which precedes and underpins them. Overlapping with both these areas of uncertainty are the specific conundrums involved with the alleged universality of human rights at a time when individual and group diversity is also a prized value.

These philosophical problems should not be ignored because they are expressed in an abstract and theoretical manner. Putting such issues to one side because there is general agreement that there is a role for human rights discourse in contemporary political systems ignores the practical problems which arise from genuine controversy over the content and form of human rights. Many questionable constitutional arguments are put forward by people who simply assume that we can know in advance what human rights are and have only to determine how best they may be enforced and promoted. Pronouncements are routinely made about the relative merits of courts and assemblies as guardians of human rights on the basis that we can inspect the outcomes of both approaches and observe which better

13

secures the assumed objectives.[14] Yet, without a prior consensus as to precisely what these objectives are, which would require agreement at a level of specificity which is precise enough to guide conduct, such arguments carry little weight. In the absence of such consensus every constitutional recommendation must be made on the premise of the inherently controversial nature of the content and form of human rights at the level of implementation. Consensus on generalized standards and abstract affirmations is an inadequate basis for recommending any particular mechanism for the articulation and realization of human rights.

The epistemological and ontological deficits of human rights not only undermine superficial arguments in favour of this or that method of institutionalizing rights, but are manifest in the increasing controversiality of judicial decisions in the human rights field. It is the philosophical problems of human rights which explain the practical difficulties encountered in the attempts of courts and governments to reach evidently correct and widely accepted interpretations of fundamental rights in such realms as human reproduction, criminal law and procedure, positive discrimination, euthanasia, racial vilification, and pornography.

There are practical solutions to these philosophical problems. These involve giving identifiable persons the authority to determine the meaning to be ascribed to human rights as they are to be applied. Human rights then become what specified courts, referenda or parliaments say they are. Disagreement is overcome by constitutionally authorized decision-making. Human rights, in the specific meaning in which they have application to actual social circumstances, are what the validating authority determines. Such positivization of abstract human rights greatly assists their implementation, but the very act of concretizing rights undermines their moral authority and reduces their capacity to provide a basis for external assessments of the workings of legal and political systems.

The continuing and exponential growth of human rights institutionalization illustrates these pragmatic solutions to some of the theoretical problems. There may be no acceptable epistemology of human rights but once we have positive rules and principles carrying the authorized human rights label then we can deploy familiar methods of legal reasoning to come to a determination of the content of human rights. We can then ascribe to human rights such ontological status as we ascribe to positive law in general. In this way, the development of human rights as a political and legal process appears to by-pass philosophical anxieties. Yet, as we institutionalize human rights, they become just another set of rules and principles and just another set of human organizations which embody just another set of negotiated and enforced compromises between the dominant values of the time.

14 An example is S. Freeman, 'Constitutional Democracy and the Legitimacy of Judicial Review' (1990) 9 *Law and Philosophy* 327. The appropriate critique is well made in J. Waldron, 'Freeman's Defense of Judicial Review' (1994) 13 *Law and Philosophy* 27.

14

Positivizing human rights undermines the power of the concept to provide a source of morally imperious critiques of ordinary laws and legal systems. The robustness of conflicting analyses of human rights makes it clear that neither the content nor the form of such rights as we wish to identify as 'human' or 'fundamental' are uncontroversial. Nor is there any methodology that can provide a more objective or more convincing way of settling these controversies than is available in the case of attempts to settle disagreements about any other set of rights and duties. Human rights, as positivized in conventions, codes or bills, have the potential to be used for or against the particular very different ideals treasured by all those who are prepared to sign up to some highly generalized commitments to human liberty, equality, and well-being. Everything depends on precisely how the abstractions are given precision in relation to specific fact situations and how this is to be done cannot be deduced from the concept of human rights itself.

The basis of philosophical criticism of the idea of human rights has not been hostility to promoting the ideals of equality, liberty, and the rule of law, nor has it involved rejecting the analytical and political goals of giving these rhetorical conceptions increased clarity and specificity. Rather, the basic criticism is that the identification and articulation of human rights in a form in which they have some application to real-life circumstances is an inherently difficult and controversial matter on which rational individuals, even from within the same culture, can radically disagree. There are major choices to be made about what sort of rights we want, in form, content, and application. Philosophical criticism is targeted at a naive universalism which confuses agreement on vague statements of principle and evocations of positive emotional responses to abstract verbal formula with consensus as to how we ought to treat each other in practice and what sort of political and economic conduct is unacceptable. This basic criticism can take many different forms.

Thus, individual rights may be analysed in ways which demonstrate that agreement on the same formula masks disagreement about the meaning of that formula. The right to life is taken by some to mean the right not to be killed in any circumstance, thus excluding capital punishment and compulsory military service, and by others it is hedged around with numerous provisos and exceptions which legitimate the use of lethal force. For some people the right to life applies to all stages and forms of human life, from conception through to brain-stem death in a living body. Others prefer a qualitative definition of the sort of human life to which we have a right, involving a certain level of consciousness and/or capacity for thought and choice. There are those who interpret the right to life as the right not to be killed and those who see it as mandating the provision of the necessities of life, including adequate sustenance and medical care. Such differences of view amongst those who concur in affirming 'the' right to life can be traced to differing philosophical and political views, none of which exclude endorsing human rights as the basis of humane treatment and political legitimacy

15

and none of which contravenes the standard catch phrases of 'human dignity' or 'equal concern and respect'.

Epistemological approaches to the critique of naive universalism concentrate on demonstrating the theoretical and practical difficulties of establishing a way of selecting the content and form of rights. To survey this field would be to take in the whole moral philosophy which may be seen as a cyclical history of failed attempts to establish an objective basis for moral judgement which has a foundation beyond the appeal to the norms of an established culture. The strongest argument in favour of moral objectivity has always been the felt certainty of selected moral 'intuitions'. The insurmountable objection to the appeal to subjective certainty has always been the diverse content to which such certainty adheres.[15]

In recent times the search for a universal foundation for moral norms has manifested itself in the attempt to establish an agreed basis in certain aspect of moral experience, such as basic rights, and concede irreversible diversity on other moral topics, such as the content of the good life. The objective is to identify a limited scope for justice or human rights, a core of self-evident foundational rights which can be set apart from politics and exempted from the subjectivist critique. If successful, this approach has profound political implications since it suggests that determinations of basic rights can be attained by a suitably impartial élite, while leaving the details of the good life to be worked out in the wider democratic process.

Unsurprisingly, the most powerful versions of the distinctive epistemology of rights are the products of a jurisdiction with a long history of an entrenched Bill of Rights. The most audacious effort in this regard is Rawls's rather short-lived claim to have revived the classical enlightenment methodologies to the point of providing a way of reaching justified agreement with respect to justice, including the content of fundamental rights.[16] Interestingly, it was in the period when the Rawls-led return to substantive political philosophy was rehabilitated after the sceptical critiques of linguistic philosophers that academic defences of universal human rights re-emerged to give legitimacy to those who sought to commend a non-ideological consensus on human rights which could and should be extracted from the mess of actual politics.

Not much remains in current moral and political philosophy of the claims to provide a reliable epistemology of rights. Rawls has retreated to redescribe his theory as a pragmatic political technique within a certain type of liberal state.[17] In the legal community, however, there is still considerable attachment to Ronald Dworkin's version of the distinction between the right and the good according to which there are matters of fundamental principle that

15 The best brief account of this debate is to be found in J.L. Mackie, *Ethics: Inventing Right and Wrong* (1977).
16 J. Rawls, *A Theory of Justice* (1971) marked the restoration of confidence in Kantian style methods as a means to obtaining objective consensus on basic rights and has had an important justificatory role in many defences of judicial review of legislative action.
17 J. Rawls, *Political Liberalism* (1993).

16

are at base matters of individual rights which manifest the principle of equal concern and respect and are logically distinct from the valuations which focus on desirable outcomes of public policy.[18] In Dworkin's analysis, principles and rights have epistemological and therefore constitutional priority over competing views of the good life about which politicians and citizens may reasonably be left to contend. Dworkin's approach is saved from the unimaginable abstractions of Rawls's hypothetical original position, from which we are intended to construct the content of basic rights, by being historically tied to the progressive articulation of law within actual jurisdictions. His basic rights are constructed from an interpretation of particular legal traditions. From the point of view of human rights, however, this compromises the moral independence of the rights, for they are tied to the contingencies of a particular culture. Congruence with even selected strains from a specific legal history does not cut much philosophical ice as a basis for choice of rights within that jurisdiction, let alone in relation to trans-cultural objectivity.

The most promising theories of objectivist moral epistemology have been those which focus on information, choice, and impartiality. The compelling attraction of Rawls's initial theory of justice as fairness derived from the way in which it associates preferred moral norms with being better informed, freely chosen, and impartially arrived at. However, while moral judgements based on factual error can be rejected, information is in itself the object rather than the origin of moral judgement, for such judgement is an assertion of the acceptability or otherwise of certain states of affairs. Similarly, choice cannot in itself be a test of moral rightness since particular choices are themselves objects of moral assessment. Only the formal qualities of certain choices, such as its impartiality, can endow choice with moral status with respect to the content of that choice. By default, therefore, impartiality becomes the key category in the attempt to provide objective bases for moral judgement, and impartiality is certainly a powerful idea with respect to the acceptability of moral judgements. Indeed, there is a good case for taking impartiality as a defining feature of morality, in that it is possible to classify an individual's preference for herself as amoral as well as immoral unless equivalent self-preference is allowed to all similar persons. Hence the continuing force of Kant's universalizability principle.

Yet, the long history of critique of Kant's position and the shorter but more intense examination of Rawls's theory amply demonstrate that there is more to morality than impartiality. Partiality for one person or group of persons over another may exclude some putative moral positions as simply selfish, but such impartiality is compatible with an infinity of different evaluative commitments. Impartiality may take us as far as equality of rights

---

18 The basic constitutional implications of Dworkinian jurisprudence are made clear in his influential essay, R. Dworkin, *A Bill of Rights for Britain* (1990). See, also, his *Freedom's Law: The Moral Reading of the American Constitution* (1996).

but it does not get to the core of which rights are to be allocated on a basis of equality. Information, choice, and impartiality may be essential ingredients in progressing moral belief systems; they do not in themselves settle any significant value disagreements.

The fact that human rights have flourished without sustained philosophical approval may be taken to prove the perennial appeal of the former and the general irrelevance of the latter. However, the philosophical scepticism concerning naive enthusiasm for allegedly apolitical human rights is in no way undermined by their political popularity. The theoretical problems identified by critical philosophers manifest themselves in real life controversies which threaten the usefulness and stability of human rights regimes.

IDEOLOGY AND HUMAN RIGHTS

The international growth of the human rights movement since the end of the Second World War has been phenomenal with respect to its ideological acceptance if not in relation to international compliance with its standards. This growth has come about alongside and despite consistent criticism of the philosophical base of key concept: the idea of universal, inalienable individual rights which have the epistemological characteristic of self-evidence, in that their content and form are inherently uncontroversial amongst reasonable people.

The moral power of the human rights ideology derives from the consensus that there are certain things that people have done to each other in the course of human history which are atrocious and ought not to be repeated. What may be called the torture paradigm connects human rights with a shared perception of totally unacceptable evils which are never justified and undermine the claims to political legitimacy of any system of government.[19] The constitutional insight of the human rights movement is that the determination of when these atrocities have been committed cannot be left to governments themselves, since they have been the prime perpetrators. On the torture paradigm of human rights, setting up a superior court to adjudicate on the evils perpetrated by government seems warranted as a mechanism of accountability through procedurally acceptable findings of fact.

Yet the scope of human rights has, with good reason, been extended beyond a few apparently uncontroversial evils characteristically brought about by the power of governments, and now covers a broad range of social, civil, political, and economic interests which impact on every aspect of life in a modern society. Moreover, such rights are analysed as involving correlative

19 This is not to say that the question of what constitutes torture from the perspective of human rights is uncontested. See C. MacKinnon, 'On Torture: A Feminist Perspective on Human Rights' in *Human Rights in the Twenty-First Century: A Global Challenge*, eds. K. Mahoney and P. Mahoney (1992) 21.

18

duties that call for positive actions to secure the identified interests.[20] Thus, the human right to health not only prioritizes health interests but places burdens on government to ensure that basic health care is available to all on the basis of medical need, irrespective of capacity to pay, and affirms that claims based on such rights have equal valence to other human rights based interests. What may be called the health paradigm of human rights develops not only the content of human rights in the direction of well-being but also, in the shift from negative to positive rights, alters their form, and, with respect to relative importance in the deployment of scarce resources, their valence.[21]

The torture paradigm differs from the health paradigm not only with respect to the content and form of the rights to be protected but in relation to the dynamic of the human rights enterprise. On the torture paradigm the emphasis is on achieving conformity to agreed minimal standards of conduct, such as the elimination of torture. The health paradigm is more of a developmental model which sees the role of human rights institutions domestically to be one of progressive development of law and social attitudes with respect to human equalities and the realization of fundamental human interests, but nevertheless insisting on the imperative force of a basic minimum of achievement in relation to the available resources of the society. The health care paradigm is misrepresented when it is considered merely aspirational for it relates not simply to ideals of a desirable form of social life, but represents genuine attempts to identify minimal acceptabilities of equal import to the original civil and political rights.

The shift to the health paradigm gives normality to the idea that all rights are costly to protect and brings a different emphasis to the interpretation and enforcement of civil and political rights, emphasizing, for instance, that legal aid may be as much a prerequisite of a fair trial as the assumption of innocence. This fusion of the torture and health models of human rights serves to identify not simply the priority but the required goals for democratic governments. In total, the combination of torture and health care models require a society which is, for instance, free of discrimination, committed to the equal development of all, makes decisions only after open discussion, holds fair and open elections, and provides for quality education, culture, and health care. Human rights thus become highly inclusive, omitting little that may be identified as a fundamental human interest. Moreover, there is nothing in the concept of human rights other than the perceived importance of the rights in question to bring to a close extensions of the scope of the domain of human rights from the torture to the health paradigm. Thus, in the international sphere we have already moved beyond social, economic, and cultural rights to what is referred to as a third tier of

20 See M. Menlowe and A. McCall Smith (eds.), *A Duty to Rescue* (1993).
21 These themes are explored in V.A. Leay, 'Implications of a Right to Health' in Mahoney and Mahoney, op. cit., n. 19.

19

human rights, involving collective rights to such matters as development and environmental enhancement.[22]

While the progressive move towards equalizing the importance of torture and health paradigms lends credibility to the ideological neutrality of rights discourse, it does exacerbate the epistemological problem of identifying the proper mode for determining the content, form, and valence of such rights. Moreover, it produces intractable decision-problems in settling the inevitable clashes between rights and how far they are defeasible in the light of economic and political circumstances. Controversies of this sort reach a degree of sustained disagreement to the point where it seems reasonable to despair of the rights-approach as an appropriate way to institutionalize the settlement of value disputes in society. Certainly, the task of monitoring and applying rights is overtaken by the need to determine their content, form, and valence. In these circumstances, there must be heightened concerns about locating the articulation and development of such abstract rights in judicial organs, whose impartiality may enhance their capacity to make independent findings of fact and apply existing law but in no way qualifies them to make value judgements on behalf of the community.

CONSTITUTING HUMAN RIGHTS

The superior mystique of human rights is such that they have been regarded as being in a class of their own as in some way an exception to the contestability of other normative choices. If this is not the case then there is every reason to be cautious about exempting human rights from the normal processes of democratic scrutiny. For, while it may be an excellent strategy for the furtherance of equality, liberty, and well-being to identify certain laws as more fundamental than others in that the community wishes to give them priority over any other norms with which they may come into conflict, we have noted that we cannot assume that there is some special epistemological access to human rights which makes it safe to abrogate their articulation to an entrenched legal process. There may be other more sceptical but ultimately more efficacious methods of giving institutional expression to the insight that it is important to identify and protect fundamental human interests and ensure that these are not lost sight of in the give and take of everyday politics.

22 These 'third generation' rights are not, so far, serious contenders for inclusion in justiciable human rights law, but there is no reason why, for instance, the right of non-nationals to humanitarian assistance, or certain environmental rights, should not be a candidates for juristic human rights and given equal weight to certain civil and political rights ('first generation') and most economic and social rights ('second generation'). For the terminology, see K. Vasak, *'Les differentes categories des Droits de l'Homme'* in *Les Dimensiones Universelles des Droits de l'Homme*, vol. 2, eds. A. Lapeyre et al. (1990) 297.

20

Constitutional questions focus specifically on who should exercise which political powers in a jurisdiction, with legal interest centring on the separation of powers, particularly between legislative and judicial power. We have seen that there is reason to doubt whether there is a readily delineable domain of human rights which can safely be assumed to be insufficiently controversial to excise from the electorally-oriented political systems of democratic accountability. Institutions set up to enforce the self-evident rights of citizens are not fitted to the role of deciding what the content and valence of these rights is to be. Yet, instead of being tribunals primarily to determine questions of fact as to human rights violations, human rights courts have become *de facto* legislatures, able to determine what is and what is not to count as a violation of human rights. While it seems intuitively right that we cannot entrust safeguarding democracy to those who currently hold elective office, since they have an evident interest in subverting the democratic process in order to retain and enhance their existing power, it seems equally clear that there is no reason why élite legal opinion as to the practical import of abstract rights should be allowed to determine what is and what is not democratic. Moreover, given the ever enlarging scope of human rights, court-based entrenchment of human rights in general is even more incongruous when this involves judicial settlement of political priorities in so many areas of political disagreement.

It is not suggested that there are easy solutions to these problems. The problem of guarding the guardians is as old as political philosophy itself. As Hobbes so graphically identified, human societies suffer the tragic fate of being vulnerable to the political and economic organizations on which they depend. We must expect, therefore, that there are intractable antinomies at the core of choices about institutionalizing human rights. It is always possible to find good arguments against locating bottom-line power to any one locus or combination of loci. Protecting minorities seems to require endangering the legitimate interests of majorities and other minorities. Forms of entrenchment which require large majorities are ineffective with respect to the protection of highly unpopular minorities, intolerance often being enhanced by a dominant consensus. We may distrust politicians because they have short-term objectives and vested interests in the denial of democratic rights, but we may have more problems with the rule of lawyers, a somewhat despised occupational group with a proven record of professional self-interest. Judiciaries are normally excepted from this low esteem, but where they are given major political powers, their decisions come under public scrutiny and their special expertise (in the law) is questioned as the exclusive criterion of appointment. Given reasonable laws, judges are accepted as socially beneficial while they act positivistically, but not otherwise.[23] If we then go to the people by way of referenda, we arrive at the

23 This theme is developed in T. Campbell, 'Legal Positivism and Political Power' in *Political Theory: Tradition and Diversity*, ed. A.Vincent (1997) 172–9.

21

antithesis of the protection of minorities. Populist views on the specifics of social issues are rarely in accordance with the goals of most human rights activists. Yet, consent in some form must be the ultimate foundation of all political legitimacy.

These difficult choices are all manifest in the institutionalization of human rights. If we retain only relatively costless negative rights then we under-emphasize social and economic interests. If we stress basic social and economic interests as equally significant human rights, then we take judges into areas with which they are not equipped to deal and give them power over resources for which they are not responsible. If we seek to positivize human rights in a manner which accords with a version of the rule of law which favours predictability, uniformity, and impartiality in applying and securing human rights, then the higher law becomes ordinary law, subject to all the weaknesses of over- and under-inclusiveness, legalism, and inflex-ibility. If we leave human rights as open-ended invitations to the exercise of moral judgement by the current legal authorities, this undermines the useful-ness of the legal system in providing a stable framework of expectations and remedies. If we emphasize the symbolism of rights, the importance they have for education, and the political impact they can have on political emotions, we need broadly based inclusive statements of rights which are of little use in generating justiciable tests of political legitimacy.

Ultimately, the formalities of a constitutional regime may be of secondary importance to the development of a culture of democracy in which there is a degree of commitment to open dialogue and compromise as well as a real-ization that, while acceptance of majority opinion may be the best closure mechanism for political disagreements, this lacks legitimacy if the majority seriously neglects the sort of claims which underlie the development of human rights law. Indeed, the principal significance of the choice of consti-tutional mechanisms may be their impact on such a democratic culture as the only enduring defence against authoritarianism and abuse. From this point of view, institutionalizing human rights may be important mainly because of the ways in which it symbolizes the inadequacies of pure majori-tiarianism, gives focus for the formation of public opinion on the basic interests of all citizens, and provides mechanisms for addressing individual grievances, objectives which may be met without formalizing a counter-majoritarian veto on the electoral political procedures. The question is whether this can be achieved without giving too much influence to a globalized network of judicial authorities to the detriment of healthy representative politics.

THE HUMAN RIGHTS ACT

These reflections range far beyond the relatively modest step of incorporating the European Convention on Human Rights in the mild way envisaged in

22

the Human Rights Act, an Act which is concerned principally with interpretation of domestic law, not with its replacement. However, it may not be easy to restrict the impact of the Act to minor questions of interpretation. Interpretation is itself a slippery term which is now used much more widely than simply in relation to making a selection between different readings of ambiguous statements, and is often equated with highly flexible forms of legal reasoning.[24] Interpretation may involve creative concretizations of vague statements in order to give justiciable meaning to those statements, a process which goes far beyond resolving ambiguities.[25] With respect to more specific statements of rights, 'interpretation' is taken to include how we read legal texts to determine whether or not there is an ambiguity which needs to be addressed as well as the process of resolving that ambiguity. The attempt to distance the ECHR from making or unmaking United Kingdom law and confining its use to the clarification of obscurities comes up against the thesis that obscurity is not something which comes on the face of a statement but emerges from the pre-existing state of mind of those who seek to give meaning to a form of words.

Although these points may be overstated in that they ignore the existence of relatively stable understandings of verbal patterns within particular cultures, there is no doubt that the existence of the ECHR does impact on how we read our domestic laws in the first place. The Convention affects what seems clear and what does not as well as which clarifications are to be preferred. And so, while it is possible to sustain a fair working distinction between understanding and interpretation in a legal culture where there is sufficient precision and continuity of discourse, this process is undermined by the introduction of unspecific principles as a guide to the so-called interpretation of pre-identified ambiguities and obscurities.

Further, it is not clear what will be made of the requirement of s. 6 that public authorities must conform to the ECHR. This may be read (or 'interpreted') as permitting or even requiring courts, which are explicitly identified in the Act as public authorities, to develop the common law so that it is increasingly in harmony with the Convention. This may not be the intention of the Act's sponsors, but, in a fluid constitutional situation involving the

---

24 See A. Marmor (ed.), *Interpretation and Legal Theory* (1992) and B. Bix (ed.), *Law, Language and Legal Determinacy* (1993).

25 This and related problems are examined in an important article that casts doubt on the utility and clarity of the model on which much of the Human Rights Act is based: A.S. Butler, 'The Bill of Rights Debate: Why the New Zealand Bill of Rights Act 1990 is a Bad Model for Britain' (1997) 17 *Oxford J. of Legal Studies* 323. See, also, G. Huscroft and P. Rishworth (eds.), *Rights and Freedoms: The New Zealand Bill of Rights Act 1990 and the Human Rights Act 1993* (1995), and J. Elkind, 'New Zealand's Experience with a Non-Entrenched Bill of Rights' in *Towards an Australian Bill of Rights*, ed. P. Alston (1994) 235. S. 6 of the New Zealand Bill of Rights Act reads: '6. Interpretation consistent with Bill of Rights to be preferred – Wherever an enactment can be given a meaning consistent with the rights and freedoms contained in this Bill of Rights, the meaning shall be preferred to any other meaning'.

changing role of courts, it is possible that judiciaries will modify their working assumptions as to how statutes, including the Human Rights Act, are to be interpreted. Certainly, there are available theories of interpretation, particularly in the human rights sphere, which place few limitations on judges' power to understand the enactments of legislature in accordance with generalized norms which permit cognizance of purposes other than those in the mind of the legislators.

Putting these two points together, if British judiciaries choose to develop the common law in accordance with the precedents established in the European Court of Human Rights and the decisions of the Commission, and if they systematically 'interpret' any parliamentary modifications of the common law in such a way as to make them compatible with the ECHR, there is little than can be demonstrated to be legally wrong in their conduct. We could therefore have a situation where there is increased impetus to develop the common law without the sense of illegitimacy that at present accompanies significant changes unapproved by Parliament, and will decreased the legal and political capacity of Parliament to exercise its theoretical sovereignty by passing legislation which can decisively override common law developments.

It is argued that this will not happen. In support it is pointed out that current decisions of the European Court are not threatening in this way and that there is no will on the part of the British judiciaries to take on such wider powers. This may well be so in the short term, but relatively small constitutional changes have to be seen against the wider process of change, and we cannot easily extrapolate from current decisions and attitudes to what will be the case in ten, twenty or fifty years time. This might not matter if the constitutional changes are readily reversible as is the case under the doctrine of the sovereignty of Parliament. However, what may emerge is a process of entrenchment whereby reversibility is disallowed or made more difficult. Already, the sovereignty of Parliament is no longer a fixed point of British constitutional law. It therefore becomes imperative to look at possible long-term consequences under different legal cultures, different judiciaries, and different political situations, noting that some of these differences will themselves be the result of promoting a juridification of political issues by giving an ever-increasing law-making role to judges. It would appear that the Act gives encouragement to liberal methods of interpretation which have the potential to undermine the traditional ethics of adjudication which requires a basic commitment to respecting the intention of the legislature as expressed in the legislated text.

Working through these potential implications of the Act may require a new model of the separation of powers which can provide bounds within which judiciaries and legislatures can work co-operatively in a way which ensures that human rights are more at the centre of a political debate in which citizens can participate. This model requires elements of tension and partnership between the legislative, executive, and judicial branches of

24

government. An enhanced role for parliamentary committees is one emerging feature of such a model. The declaration of incompatibility outlined in s. 4 of the Act could prove to be an ingredient which helps to shape the political agenda and attract parliamentary and media attention in a way which improves the quality of political discourse and encourages a human-rights-centred focus for constitutional partnership. In such ways, the Human Rights Act may be an enduringly beneficial constitutional development which contributes to a relatively stable and sensible model of the relative roles of judges, parliamentarians, and populace in the identification and development of what the community elects to identify as human rights.

CONCLUSION: A CULTURE OF CONTROVERSY

This essay has taken an overview of the Human Rights Act in the context of the potential of human rights institutionalization. It suggests that the Act may help to produce a framework which is compatible with the continuing centrality of Parliament as the core democratic institution. It is accepted that any satisfactory contemporary constitutional arrangement is dependent on a widespread acceptance of the idea of human rights as central to political legitimacy, but this must involve the awareness that the content, form, and valence of human rights are inherently controversial so that any satisfactory regime of human rights must be the product of continuing debate, with respect to the precise formulation of human rights law, to which citizens and their representatives are the major contributors.

Effectively highlighting the importance of identifying and protecting fundamental human interests does require a generally understood culture of rights. However, we have seen that this need not mean accepting an ethos of narrow self-interest which excludes a commitment to the public goods on which most fundamental human interests depend. Legitimate self-interest incorporates a degree of reciprocation and can even accommodate a degree of altruism. We have also seen that a culture of rights need not involve looking principally to courts rather than to representative politics for solutions to value disagreements and competing interests. In fact, it may require that courts be seen as essentially protectors rather than definers of rights, providing remedies on the basis of proven violations of existing positive rights as enunciated elsewhere. A human rights culture need not be a culture of litigation any more than it has to be a culture of dependence, a matter of looking to others rather than ourselves for solutions to our problems on the grounds that protecting our interests is primarily a duty of others rather than an achievement for ourselves. A culture of rights may be political rather than legal in its nature, preferring debate to litigation and voting in representative assemblies to voting in the court room, particularly when fundamental interests are at stake.

25

Seeing human rights as a vital part of a culture of controversy in which neither parliaments, courts or the people are to be trusted, and in which the core of politics must be oriented to reaching a series of legally enforceable but temporary agreements as to the rights which best protect and enhance the equal interests of all citizens, may enable us to view the Human Rights Act as a useful development which gives further institutional recognition to a democratic style of human rights regime in which parliaments and electorates are encouraged to address human rights questions in an involved and responsible manner.

26

JOURNAL OF LAW AND SOCIETY
VOLUME 26, NUMBER 1, MARCH 1999
ISSN: 0263-323X, pp. 27-37

The Politics of the Human Rights Act

JAMES YOUNG*

The Human Rights Act is the result of post-war changes in Europe. It is the consequence less of the campaigning of dedicated individuals and more of the change in the position of the United Kingdom in Europe and the world. Objections to incorporation of the Convention have given way to the desire to be like the rest of Europe. Traditional views of the judicial role have given way to a perception of the judiciary as the last bastion against an over-powerful executive, unchecked by Parliament.

INTRODUCTION

It is, I suppose, inevitable that for political reasons we must – in some form of other – accept this draft Convention. At the same time I feel bound to state that from the point of view of administration of the law I regard this necessity as an unqualified misfortune.[1]

I chair many Cabinet committees, but none that has given me greater satisfaction than the committee whose labours have brought this Bill forward in the first legislative Session. It occupies a central position in our integrated programme for constitutional change.[2]

The change of perspective has something to do, no doubt, with the person-alities of these two men: Lord Jowitt, something of a little Englander with a conservative attitude towards the common law, Lord Irvine, an expansive European. Yet Jowitt expressed especially forceful arguments which were widely held then and later. The reason for the change in the thinking of the political élite, of course, is to do with the changing socio-political landscape since 1950. It is these changes and the responses to them which form the basis of this essay.

---

1 Memorandum to the Cabinet, CAB 130/64 [appendix to GEN 337/1st meeting], cited in G. Marston, 'The United Kingdom's Part in the Preparation of the European Convention on Human Rights' (1993) 42 *International and Comparative Law Q.* 796.
2 Lord Irvine, 58 *H.L. Debs.*, col. 1227 (3 November 1997).

* *Lecturer in Law, Cardiff Law School, P.O Box 427, Museum Avenue, Cardiff CF1 1XD, Wales*

The two 'progenitors'[4] of the Convention were the Universal Declaration of Human Rights[5] of 1948 and a draft Convention produced by the European Movement. The Universal Declaration was not and is not binding on states. It was a direct response to the outrages of the Second World War and contains a declaration of Human Rights in generally absolute terms, not hedged around by many reservations and exceptions, as the European Convention was to be. The Universal Declaration also goes further than the protection of traditional negative civil and political freedoms. It includes the rights to work, to rest, to social security, to an adequate standard of living, and to education.[6] As it was not legally binding, it could have no enforcement machinery.[7] The European Movement was a non-governmental organization, but it included some influential European politicians. While the Universal Declaration was aspirational, the draft Convention made provision for a European Court which would determine whether states had breached the Convention.

The Council of Europe was established in 1949.[8] Already, the Convention was controversial. The idea for the Council of Europe was regarded with suspicion by the Labour government, which was keen to avoid attempts to make the Council of Europe the precursor of European integration.[9] Bevin, the Foreign Secretary, opposed a European parliament, seeing the Council as a forum for consultation between ministers of sovereign states. The Consultative Assembly which was eventually enshrined in the Statute of the Council of Europe was a concession to those who wanted a parliament,[10] but the central role of the Committee of Ministers enabled integrationist ambitions to be contained. There were those, including some British politicians, who had aspirations which have not yet been realized in the European Union. Churchill, to the embarrassment of some of his ardent late-twentieth-century admirers, championed a move towards a federative system, including a European army.[11]

---

3 Marston, op. cit., n. 1.
4 A.H. Robertson, *Human Rights in Europe* (1963) 7.
5 U.N. doc. A/811.
6 id., articles 23, 24, 22, 25, 26.
7 The International Covenant, and so on, were to follow and provide some form of accountability.
8 See C. Archer, *Organising Europe* (1994) 57–60; A.H. Robertson, *The Council of Europe: Its Structure, Functions and Achievements* (1956) ch. 1.
9 See his forthright attack on those who had such ambitions in 480 *H.C. Debs.*, cols. 1500–02 (13 November 1950).
10 Although this is now known as the Parliamentary Assembly of the Council of Europe, the representatives from the each member state are chosen from among members of the national parliament to reflect the political balance therein and retains a primarily consultative function.
11 See M. Gilbert, *Winston Churchill 1945–1965*, vol VIII (1988) 541–3.

28

The resistance to the Convention from British governments started with the drafting of the Convention. A future Conservative Lord Chancellor took an active part in the drafting of the Convention – an inversion of today's politics. As the quotation at the beginning of this essay shows, Lord Jowitt saw the Convention as a threat to the English common law and to the liberties of English law.[12] In the end he was forced to accept it. However, he did get his way in important respects. First, the rights under the Convention are hedged around with exceptions and reservations. Some were clearly introduced to safeguard existing English legal provisions.[13] Secondly, certain rights were excluded from the Convention, in particular, the right of property. This was seen by the Labour government as inimical to a planned socialist economy, particularly nationalization. The right was introduced later as part of Protocol 1, which the Conservative government had no difficulty in ratifying.[14] Most importantly, the British government won the concession that acceptance of the enforcement machinery was to be optional. Thus, the right of an individual to petition the European Commission of Human Rights and the compulsory jurisdiction of the European Court of Human Rights were optional.

ARGUMENTS AGAINST MAKING THE CONVENTION ENFORCEABLE

One of the striking things about the history of the debate about a Bill of Rights, and in particular, the incorporation of the European Convention, is that the basic arguments against making the Convention enforceable have changed little over time. The arguments deployed against the Convention's having an enforcement machinery have been basically similar to those against the acceptance of the right of individual petition and then against incorporation. The arguments for acceptance have perhaps changed more.

One set of arguments is based on a Diceyan tradition of what Loughlin[15] has called conservative normativism, in which important themes are 'anti-rationalism, the importance of tradition, and the value of practical experience'.[16] In this context the main arguments are that the common law, based

12 See the discussions in Marston, op. cit., n. 1, pp. 815–19; A. Lester, 'Fundamental Rights: The United Kingdom Isolated?' [1984] *Public Law* 46, 51–3.
13 For example, the protection of the law of contempt of court as a justified interference with freedom of expression in article 8 ('maintaining the authority and impartiality of the judiciary').
14 This has a public interest exception to the right to quiet enjoyment of possessions (protocol 1, art. 1).
15 M. Loughlin, *Public Law and Political Theory* (1992). Loughlin's purpose is different from mine. He is concerned to identify the strands of thought in the development of public law practice and scholarship. My concern is with the political movement towards the Human Rights Act.
16 id.

29

on accrued experience, is a better safeguard of freedoms than general statements of principle. Indeed, it is an alien tradition and would be a threat to that accrued experience. Britain, it is argued, has a longer tradition of freedom than continental European states. Parliamentary sovereignty is part of the tradition and again has proved a surer protector of freedoms in practice. It is further argued that the this would bring the judges into politics and break down the traditional separation of the legislative and judicial function. The judiciary's function is to ensure that the executive does not stray beyond the limits of the powers granted to it by Parliament or by tradition. An extension of this approach to the international law sphere was the dogmatic acceptance of the principle that only states could be the subjects of international law, and to accept the right of individual redress to a foreign tribunal would be unacceptable.

Loughlin also posits a second tradition, namely an empirical variant of functionalism. This approach in the context of the human rights debate leads to the same result, but for different reasons. It is an approach which, in the context of the bill of rights debate is associated with the political Left. The legal protection of rights is seen as the province of Parliament, because Parliament is elected, not because it is the traditional way of doing things. It is the government and Parliament which should determine how rights should be protected in response to particular needs and problems. Furthermore, the judges are not the appropriate persons to interpret general rights, since they have no democratic legitimacy, and, on one view, are conservative, white, middle- or upper-class males, whose political priorities are not representative of the population as a whole.

The arguments in favour of acceptance of the enforcement machinery of the Convention and of incorporation of the Convention are, of course, based on one or other form of liberalism.[17] They have also changed, or been added to over fifty years. The arguments are partly principled and partly concerned with diplomacy and appearances. The liberal mistrust of the state and belief in the pre-eminence of the individual has always been invoked as a basis for individual rights enforceable against the state. The justification for a Bill of Rights is the need to provide a guarantee of certain rights against interference by the executive and legislative branches of the state, regardless of their democratic legitimacy. Trust has been placed in the judiciary because they are separate from the executive and legislature and are less likely to be subject to the whims of public popularity. While it is admitted that judges will be making decisions which are political, both in the sense of being the subject of controversy between political parties and in the sense that they are the authoritative ordering of social values, this is said to be part of the judicial

17 Loughlin, id., identifies the predominant strand of thought here as 'liberal normativism'. This seems to me a less helpful way of analysing the movement for incorporation than his other 'ideal types' and so here I draw on his analysis less. There remains much acute analysis in what he writes.

30

function in any case.[18] These are the classical liberal reasons for the acceptance of a Bill of Rights. The arguments for accepting the right of petition and then incorporation are, in my view, more diverse in philosophy and pragmatically related to the historical moment.

THE JOURNEY TO INCORPORATION[19]

1. Ratifying the Convention

Variants and combinations of the arguments outlined above were used against the Convention. As long as it remained a European version of the United Nations Declaration it did not matter. What was objectionable was that these rights should be turned into enforceable rights. Arguments from conservative normativism and functionalism were intermingled in the argument put forward by those opposed to the Convention's enforcement machinery. Thus Jowitt opposed the Convention, both as a firm traditionalist adherent of the common law[20] and as a person who thought that the Convention had been drafted by an old-fashioned liberal:

> It is quite obvious to me that the draftsman, whoever he may be, starts with the standpoint of a *laissez faire* economy and has never realized that we are now living in the age of planned economy.[21]

Two further arguments were also put forward which were conservative and paternalistic. New remedies, it was argued, would be abused by meddling trouble-makers, in particular communists, who might use them to foment discord. It would be difficult not to extend the rights to colonies where the populations were too immature to be ready for the protection of such rights.[22]

18 For a useful summary of the view of judges as part of the political élite, see A. Paterson, 'Judges: A Political Elite?' (1974) 1 *Brit. J. of Law and Society* 118.
19 The use of the word 'journey' is meant only to indicate that there has been movement over a period of time. It is not intended to adhere to a Whig view of progressive history in these post-modern times.
20 A hint of xenophobia is to be found: 'We all came to the conclusion – the Attorney and Younger dissententibus – that we were not prepared to encourage our European friends to jeopardise our whole system of law, which we have laboriously built up over the centuries, in favour of some half-baked scheme to be administered by some unknown court'. LCO 2/6274 (3363/22, part 1), quoted by Marston, op. cit., n. 1, p. 813.
21 Letter to Hugh Dalton of 3 August 1950, LCO 2/5570, quoted by Lester, op. cit., n. 12, p. 51.
22 The divided authority would have dire consequences: 'Loyalty would be shaken: administration would be made more difficult and agitation more easy.' Colonial Secretary Jim Griffiths, C.P. (50) 189, CAB 129/41 34611, quoted by Lester, id., p. 50.

31

2. The campaign for individual petition

The Convention was ratified, but the British government entered reservations opting out of the right of individual petition and the compulsory jurisdiction of the Court. Thereafter there was no movement towards changing government policy. In 1951 the Conservative party won the general election and remained in office for thirteen years. Conservative normativism and functionalism were agreed. A low-level campaign was conducted in the form of backbench questions about the right of individual petition and the jurisdiction of the European Court of Human Rights. The replies given emphasized the danger of mischief-makers and the inappropriateness of individual remedies in international law.[23] There was slightly less activity in the House of Lords, which was later to become the testing-ground of the incorporation campaign.

It was not until the Labour government came to power in October 1964 that there was a change of policy. Once again it was an opposition Member of Parliament, this time a Conservative, who raised the question of the right of individual petition.[24] Despite no previous Labour party political agenda, the government response was positive. As casually as the right of individual petition had been brushed aside for thirteen years, it was accepted; there were no manifesto commitments or Cabinet discussions.[25] Yet the acceptance of the right to individual petition and the compulsory jurisdiction of the European Court of Human Rights in 1966 was an important decision.

3. The incorporation campaign

Once the right of individual petition had been accepted, then the campaign for incorporation began. There is a sense in which the fears of Lord Jowitt were vindicated. Once a foreign tribunal was given the right to adjudicate on disputes between citizen and state, the arguments for giving the power to a national court were reduced. Michael Zander has helpfully catalogued legislative attempts at incorporation.[26] Two names recur in this catalogue, Lord Wade and Lord Lester: this is instructive. The only attempts which made significant legislative progress were those in the House of Lords. This is, of course, a reflection of the fact that it is easier to introduce private members' Bills and of the less heated political party atmosphere. All the attempts failed through lack of parliamentary time and the government decision to kill the Bill in the House of Commons.

23 For example, *H.C. Debs.*, vol. 574, col. 867 (29 July 1957); vol. 595, col. 1143 (19 November 1958); vol. 596, col. 333, 26 November 1958; vol. 624, col. 173 (23 May 1960); vol. 660, col. 156 (31 May 1962); (written answer) vol. 696, col. 926 (15 June 1964).

24 Terence Higgins MP, who married in 1961 the now-distinguished international lawyer Rosalyn Higgins, now British Judge in the International Court of Justice, 704 *H.C. Debs.*, col. 1051 (22 December 1964).

25 Lester, op. cit., n. 12, p. 60.

26 M. Zander, *A Bill of Rights?* (1997).

32

Up to and including the general election of 1992, there was consensus on incorporation. Although Lord Hailsham had secured the inclusion of mention of consideration of a Bill of Rights in the Conservative manifesto of 1979, it was clearly not a priority, and the promise of inter-party co-operation led nowhere. Incorporation was of no significance to the key members of the two major political parties. Conservative rhetoric was against Europe and the Labour Party continued to take the functionalist line. 'Old Labour' and radical conservatism did not trust judges and agreed that it was Parliament, dominant in constitutional theory and controlled by the executive, of course, which must determine human rights issues. Even after thirteen years of vigorous Conservative rule, the shadow Home Secretary, Roy Hattersley[27] set his face against a general Bill of Rights and opted for legislation dealing with particular rights in 1992. The Conservative government looked to home-grown charters for customers, something like manufacturers' guarantees, rather than rights for citizens. The fact that it had been in the Liberal Democratic manifesto since 1987 was of little consequence.

Suddenly, after the surprising defeat of 1992, the Labour Party changed its view of incorporation. What decided this was John Smith MP. Quite simply, he made it part of Labour Party policy. When he had committed the party to it, the new Labour leader, Tony Blair, took it up. In one way this is not surprising. One feature of the debates on the other legislative attempts to incorporate the Convention is that it was seen as the province of lawyers. Those who introduced it and most of the speakers were lawyers. Not only was this a project of the political élite, it was the project of lawyers among that élite.

CONDITIONS OF INCORPORATION

When the Bill was passed, the main issue of incorporation was ritually opposed in the House of Lords. In the House of Commons also, the debates had the air of a symbolic dance about them. The reason for this was, in my view, twofold. The issue of principle had disappeared and the political debate had lost its conviction. A number of factors produced the change of culture which turned incorporation from unthinkable to irrelevant to a natural part of constitutional change. First, the question of incorporation was always a matter for the political élite. It did not require a great political change to incorporate. This is probably generally true of constitutional reform. While one scientific opinion poll found that 75 per cent of the population favoured a Bill of Rights, this was not a Bill of Rights founded

27 See, for example, *Guardian*, 10 June 1991 and 3 October 1991; Labour Party, *Manifesto* (1992).

33

on the European Convention;[28] rather, it was one in which social and economic rights predominated.

JUDICIAL POLITICS

If the incorporation was seen primarily as a legal question, then the attitudes of the judiciary were, *par excellence*, an indicator of this change. There is no doubt that judicial politics has been very important in the recent development of the Convention. Doubts about the competence and suitability of the judiciary have been influenced by judicial attitudes. Two things are noticeable. First, senior judges have increasingly come out in favour of giving some status to the Convention. Secondly, we know about it. From being a civil libertarian cause outside the Establishment and the party political mainstream, the Convention became respectable.

What are the processes by which this happened? First, the judiciary had the impact of the Convention forced upon them. All the successful cases before Strasbourg had, of course, failed before the courts of the United Kingdom The judges were aware of this fact. Secondly, the judiciary changed its view about the proper limits to judicial review. Conventional wisdom now sees the development of judicial review in the 1960s and 1970s as judicial reaction to the desire to limit government. Conservative normativism asserted itself to control government actions.[29] The judges were reacting to the protection of individual rights against the possibilities of socialist intervention. In the 1980s and 1990s the judges and politicians became aware of the virtue of control of radical conservative governments. In a number of cases, culminating in *R. v. Secretary of State for Foreign Affairs, ex parte World Development Movement Ltd*,[30] the courts extended the basis of *locus standi*. Initially, this was done on the grounds that an organization could be have a sufficient interest in a representative capacity. This was extended then to organizations on the grounds that this was necessary to ensure the vindication of the rule of law and to make government accountable. The importance of this completion of a change of perspective cannot be overestimated. It ended the courts' deference to the special relationship between Minister and Parliament, the absolute deference to the constitutional relationship between Minister and Parliament declared in *Carltona Ltd. v. Commissioners*

---

28 The Rowntree Reform Trust poll quoted in House of Lords debates showed 76 per cent in favour of a Bill of Rights. However, their idea of a Bill of Rights was headed by the right to free hospital treatment and was primarily a Bill of social and economic rights. See S. Weir and K. Boyle, 'Human Rights in the UK' (1997) 68 *Political Q.* 128.

29 S. Sedley, 'Law and State Power: A Time for Reconstruction' (1990) 17 *J. of Law and Society* 234.

30 [1995] 1 All E.R. 611, [1995] 1 W.L.R. 386.

34

of Works.[31] If anyone believed in the effectiveness of Parliament as a check on wayward ministers, the Scott report put paid to that.

Thirdly, the judges have become used to law from alien traditions. European law has forced the judges to come to terms with different legal traditions, different approaches to precedent, different approaches to statutory interpretation. *Pepper* v. *Hart* can be seen in this context.[32]

Fourthly, the judges have not only changed their views, they have been freer to manifest their opinions. When Lord Scarman voiced his views in favour of the incorporation of the European convention in his Hamlyn Lectures in 1974, one of the remarkable features was that a judge was expressing this view. Judicial contributions to academic literature were not extensive. In some areas traditionally regarded as technical law, judges were active. Outside this, there was relatively little and what there was was not so controversial. The Kilmuir rules reinforced this natural judicial reticence to get into areas of policy when not giving judgments in court. Although they were only concerned with the broadcasting media, there is no doubt that they reflected a reticence to become involved in political controversy. It is perhaps worth quoting a short passage to give a flavour of the rules to illustrate the distance that separates the 1950s from the 1990s. The 'rules' in the form of a letter to the Director General of the BBC concerning the possible participation of judges in a series of radio lectures on the subject of 'eminent judges of the past'.[33] The rules stated:

> My colleagues and I . . . are agreed that as a general rule it is undesirable for members of the Judiciary to broadcast on the wireless or to appear on television. We recognise, however, that there may be occasions, for example, charitable appeals, when no exception could be taken to a broadcast by a Judge. We consider that if Judges are approached by the broadcasting authorities with a request to take part in a broadcast on some special occasion, the Judge concerned ought to consult the Lord Chancellor, who would always be ready to express his opinion on the particular request.

The justification for these rules is also best captured by the flavour of the language of the time

> . . . the overriding consideration, in the opinion of myself and of my colleagues, is the importance of keeping the Judiciary in this country isolated from the controversies of the day. So long as a Judge keeps silent his reputation for wisdom and impartiality remains unassailable; but every utterance which he makes in public, except in the course of the actual performance of his judicial duties, must necessarily bring him within the focus of criticism. It would, moreover, be inappropriate for the Judiciary to be associated with any series of talks or anything which could be fairly interpreted as entertainment . . .

31 [1943] 2 All E.R. 560.
32 [1993] A.C. 593 in which the House of Lords accepted that they could look at parliamentary debates in interpreting legislation.
33 Published with a comment by A.W. Bradley in [1986] *Public Law* 383. Although the Lord Chancellor's name is attached to these rules, he did emphasize collegiality in expressing the agreed views of himself, the Lord Chief Justice (Lord Goddard), the Master of the Rolls (Sir Raymond Evershed), and the President of the Probate, Divorce and Admiralty Division (Lord Merriman).

35

Of course this did not prevent judges from writing and broadcasting, yet it reflected and reinforced a reticence. When Lord Mackay abolished the rules in 1987, he laid to rest a rule which was being put more and more in question. It may be a coincidence, but there has followed a spate of judicial lectures and writings in which judges have not been afraid to voice their views on controversies of the day. Admittedly, these are not burning issues of wide public concern, although they may be issues of controversy within the political élite. The outspoken views of members of the judiciary in debates in the House of Lords[34] have demonstrated this greater liberty in controversial issues.

The consequence of this greater freedom is that, at least among public lawyers the human rights issue has become an important and debated issue. Laws J, Sedley LJ, Lord Bingham CJ, Lord Woolf MR, and Lord Browne Wilkinson are the chief participants. Indeed it is with some trepidation that public lawyers look to leading periodicals to see yet more valuable space being taken up by judges who don't need the credit for the purposes of the national Research Assessment Exercise.

The result of this is that judges have become impatient at having to make decisions which they know or suspect will be overturned by judges on grounds which they are, formally, not entitled to consider. They have employed principles of interpretation to take account of the Convention, but have sometimes been limited by the fact that they cannot directly enforce the Convention.

CHANGES IN POLITICAL CULTURE

Inextricably related to the judicial change of perception is the broader change among the political élite. Politicians have increasingly become aware of the concrete consequences of the unincorporated European Convention.[35] Increasingly, politicians have had to decide how to react to judgments of the European Court of Human Rights. Governments have been forced to respond to judgments of the European Court of Human Rights. For any government, the stream of cases on the power of the Home Secretary in the regulation of prisons and control over incarceration of life prisoners has been unavoidable. For a Conservative administration corporal punishment in schools and control in prisons has been particularly problematic. Corporal punishment in state schools has been abolished – a great blow to some Conservative MPs. Lord Jowitt was right. The acceptance of the Convention's enforcement machinery has led to the need to change law in the United Kingdom. Like Lord Jowitt, there are those who have doubted the wisdom of those changes and the necessity for them.

34 Notably Lord Browne Wilkinson in the debates over the Criminal Justice and Public Order Bill in which he was briefed by Liberty.
35 See R. Churchill and J. Young, 'The Implementation of Judgments of the European Court of Human Rights and Decisions of the Committee of Ministers in the United Kingdom' (1991) 62 *Brit. Yearbook of International Law* 283.

36

This could lead to two possible responses. Either the United Kingdom should respond to the Convention by incorporating it and taking Article 13 seriously[36] or withdrawing from the Convention. This was apparently considered during Mrs Thatcher's first administration, but as with the post-war Labour government, diplomatic considerations outweighed principle. Where there were reservations, they have been replaced by a desire to be seen to be European. There is a persistent desire not to be seen to be left out. After 1989 the new members of the Council of Europe all have their constitutional protection of human rights. Furthermore, Canada and New Zealand have shown that the common law in established independent countries can accept a Bill of Rights. For the United Kingdom, shorn of its empire and lacking the confidence of an imperial power, the desire to be in step with the rest of the world is understandable.

CONCLUSION

In considering the cultural change, I am referring to the change in the political élite. When the Bill was introduced in 1997, the debates were a repetition of the old arguments. What had changed dramatically was the position of the advocates of incorporation. Lord Lester, the valiant champion of a lost cause, in the form of two Bills in the House of Lords, became the Lord Chancellor's spokesman. It is hard to imagine a debate in Parliament in which a person who is not a member of the government has been given so much time and deference by the Lord Chancellor. Indeed, reading the debates, one would be forgiven for thinking that there were two Lord Chancellors, Lords Irvine and Lester.

The debates of principle were over. Opposition was ritualistic. Old opponents, like Lord Donaldson, became supporters of the Bill. All that was left was the rather grubby scramble by various interest groups to get themselves excluded: the Church, the Army, the press. In all but the last, the attempts seemed to be based on misunderstandings. In all of them, the acceptance of the Convention for others verged on the hypocritical. The Human Rights Act was passed by a small political élite. It was a lawyer's provision for lawyers. It has excited lawyers. Whether this excitement will be reflected in its impact on law and politics in the United Kingdom remains to be seen.

---

36 Article 13 provides 'Everyone whose rights and freedoms as set forth in this Convention are violated shall have an effective remedy before a national authority notwithstanding that the violation has been committed by persons acting in an official capacity.

37

JOURNAL OF LAW AND SOCIETY
VOLUME 26, NUMBER 1, MARCH 1999
ISSN: 0263–323X, pp. 38–53

The European Convention as an Invigorator of Domestic Law in the Netherlands

BERT SWART*

This article examines the impact of the European Convention on Human Rights on domestic law in the Netherlands, with special regard to criminal procedure. The Convention has contributed to slow but profound transformations in the structure of criminal proceedings and to making these proceedings more adversarial and more rights oriented. It has opened up the Dutch system of criminal justice to the world and forced it to adapt itself to international standards of fairness. As a result, this system has become less naïve, more sophisticated, and more mature. Moreover, the case of the Netherlands illustrates how the Convention acts as a motor of convergence between civil law and common law systems of criminal justice.

INTRODUCTION

When the Netherlands became a party to the European Convention in 1954, the general expectation was that its impact on Dutch law and Dutch legal culture would be negligible. The prevailing opinion at that time was aptly summarized by the government during a parliamentary debate on the Bill to approve the Convention. They stated that the complex system of Dutch law offered sufficient safeguards to ensure that the principles of the Convention would be respected by the Netherlands. The view that the Convention added little or nothing to Dutch law remained predominant well into the 1960s and part of the 1970s. For instance, in 1968, an advocate general of the Dutch Supreme Court remarked that Article 6 of the European Convention was meant to protect the accused in systems of criminal justice that, unlike the Dutch system, did not pay sufficient respect to his basic rights.[1] In short, national standards of justice were held to be considerably

---

1 SC 16 January 1968, NJ 1968, 378.

* *Judge of the Court of Appeal, Amsterdam, Van Hamel Professor of International Criminal Law, University of Amsterdam, Post Box 1030, 1000 BA Amsterdam, The Netherlands*

higher than those laid down by the Convention. To argue in court that the Convention had been violated meant that one was short of better arguments.[2]

Some forty-five years after ratification of the Convention by the Netherlands it is easy to be amazed and amused by the self-complacency that reigned in the first decades after ratification. Apparently, at that time nobody was able to foresee the profound influence the European Convention would exert on the administration of justice in the Netherlands. Since then, we have become accustomed to the phenomenon that the European Court of Human Rights regularly holds the Netherlands responsible for having violated the human rights of individuals. It has also become clear that judgments of the Court in cases against other states may have major implications for Dutch law.[3] As far as the Dutch courts are concerned, they now apply the European Convention on a daily basis and they have developed a vast body of case law with regard to its provisions. In its proposals for new legislation the government will almost routinely pay attention to human rights conventions.

Not all areas of Dutch law are equally affected by the European Convention. Its impact is greatest in the fields of family law, tax law, social security law, immigration law, and, above all, criminal law. It is certainly true that, in these fields, the European Convention acts as an important invigorator of domestic law. One should even go further where criminal procedure is concerned. The European Convention lies at the basis of slow but fundamental changes in the way criminal trials are being conducted. Under the influence of the Convention, basic traditional assumptions of fairness are gradually being replaced by new ones. This is why, in this paper, I shall focus on transformations in the field of criminal procedure as a major example of what human rights conventions 'can do' to national systems of justice. Meanwhile, it is clear that, whatever part of the law one chooses to illustrate the invigorating effects of the European Convention, the Convention has contributed considerably in all areas of national law to the creation of a much stronger rights culture in the Netherlands.

THE EUROPEAN CONVENTION AND THE DUTCH CONSTITUTION

One of the main factors making the European Convention such a powerful tool in invigorating domestic law in the Netherlands lies in constitutional law.

2 For a historical overview of changing attitudes, see E. Myjer, *'Pro Justitia, Over hoe EVRM verzeild raakte in de Nederlandse strafrechtspleging en aan wie dat valt toe te rekenen'*, in *40 Jaar Europees Verdrag voor de Rechten van de Mens*, eds. A.W. Heringa et al. (1990) 270.
3 A good example is the decision of the European Court of 29 November 1988, Series A 145, in the case of *Brogan v. United Kingdom*. It led to the revision of a number of provisions in the Dutch Code of Criminal Procedure with regard to police custody. Compare A. Davenport and P. Baauw, 'Police detention in the UK and the Netherlands' in *Criminal Justice in Europe, A Comparative Study*, eds. P. Fennell et al. (1995) 253.

39

Since the beginning of the nineteenth century, the Dutch Constitution has contained a number of provisions on basic individual rights. In 1983, on the occasion of a total revision of the Constitution, these were rewritten; most of the rights of the citizen are now to be found in the first chapter of the Constitution. It is interesting to compare their content with the provisions of human rights treaties, especially the European Convention. The comparison makes it clear that, generally speaking, the Constitution does not afford broader rights protection to the individual than do human rights treaties. If there are differences, they mainly concern matters of secondary importance. The framers of the 1983 revision had been rather timid in expanding the existing constitutional rights of individual persons. Why then would the individual citizen turn to the Constitution for protection of his or her basic rights if these rights are equally, and possibly more broadly, protected by human rights treaties?

The Dutch Constitution has always forbidden the courts to test statutes passed by Parliament against the constitutional provisions on basic individual rights. In 1983, this system was preserved. Courts were, and are, only allowed to review the ordinances of lower public bodies, and this has given rise to interesting case law in some areas, the main example being the admissibility of limitations put on freedom of speech and freedom of assembly by local authorities. But apart from this limited exception, Parliament has remained the sole guardian of constitutional rights. The role of the courts is limited to examining whether or not government bodies make proper use of the powers granted to them by ordinary statutes. In the Netherlands, there is no system of constitutional review comparable to that in countries like the United States of America or the Federal Republic of Germany and, therefore, no significant body of case law on issues of constitutional law. Had there been such a system, it is likely that the European Convention would have played a more modest role in public debates on civil and political rights and liberties in the Netherlands.

Quite different is the relationship between the legislature and the courts where human rights treaties are concerned. A revision of the Constitution in 1953 widened the powers of the courts to apply the provisions of international treaties that can be considered to be self-executing. Moreover, the new constitutional provisions proclaimed the superiority of international law over national law and they explicitly recognized the power of the courts to test any national law against self-executing provisions of international treaties. Since most provisions of the European Convention as well as other human rights treaties can be considered to be self-executing, the constitutional revision of 1953 effected a fundamental change in the relationship between the legislature and the judiciary where the protection of basic individual rights is concerned. Henceforth the courts, not Parliament, would have the final say in matters touching upon these rights. All the implications of this development were certainly not foreseen at that time.

40

A national Constitution that, probably, has not more to offer than human rights treaties, a prohibition for the courts to test statutes against constitutional provisions, and new powers for them to set aside national legislation where it conflicts with the provisions of international human rights instruments: these are the main legal factors explaining why the European Convention is at the heart of most public debates on human rights and civil liberties in the Netherlands. The European Convention has become to the Dutch legal system what the national Constitution is to the legal systems of the United States of America or Germany. As a result, most provisions in the Dutch Constitution on basic individual rights tend to be neglected or overlooked. Hardly any lawyer pays systematic attention to them.

In the past decades, Dutch courts have generally been rather cautious, or sometimes even timid, in attaching consequences to the provisions of the European Convention. They tend to assume that current legislation and current practices are in conformity with the Convention unless Strasbourg case law clearly points in the opposite direction. They are followers of the case law of the European Court but rarely initiate new developments themselves. A comparison of the case law of the Dutch Supreme Court with that of the European Court makes clear that where the two courts differ in their interpretation of the Convention it is usually, although not always, the Dutch court that attaches a more limited meaning to its provisions. This is especially true in the field of criminal procedure. As a result, on a number of occasions the Supreme Court has been forced to revise its position on crucial issues of fairness in criminal proceedings, for example, the hearing of witnesses and trials in the absence of the accused, after the European Court had made it clear that it did not share the Supreme Court's view. From this I would draw the conclusion that, although the incorporation of the European Convention in Dutch law has been an important step in itself in invigorating domestic law, there is a second factor at work here: the existence of an independent international court setting European standards of respect for human rights. This is also illustrated by the fact that the impact of the International Covenant on Civil and Political Rights on Dutch law has remained very modest indeed. Moreover, in a monist system like that of the Netherlands, the rulings of the European Court have immediate effect on the daily administration of justice, national courts usually being able to follow them without any legislative intervention. On the other hand, while Dutch courts rarely anticipate Strasbourg case law, it is also true that Strasbourg has made them more rights-oriented and that leads given by the European Court have been at the basis of important developments in Dutch case law.

Not surprisingly, the impact of human rights conventions on national systems of criminal justice varies with the characteristics of these systems. For instance, a comparison of the impact of the European Convention on criminal justice in the United Kingdom and the Netherlands shows that numerous decisions have been rendered by the European Court of Human

Rights on the treatment of prisoners in the United Kingdom while such decisions are few in number where the Netherlands is concerned. On the other hand, the Court has regularly criticized the Netherlands for lack of respect for the right to a fair trial while decisions of the Court on this matter are relatively rare with regard to the United Kingdom.[4] The European Court's decisions on complaints against the Netherlands in matters of criminal law and criminal procedure mainly, though not exclusively, deal with problematic aspects of the right to a fair trial in a civil law system of justice. Six recent judgments, rendered between 1989 and 1997, in which the European Court held that the Netherlands had violated a person's right to a fair trial, well illustrate that fact.

TRADITIONAL FEATURES OF CRIMINAL JUSTICE IN THE NETHERLANDS

An analysis of the impact of the European Convention on criminal justice in the Netherlands should start with a few general remarks on the traditional features of the Dutch criminal justice system. Here, I would like to make a distinction between, on the one hand, structural factors determining the operation of the administration of criminal justice and, on the other hand, cultural factors. In this distinction, structural factors refer to the basic legal rules and assumptions governing criminal investigations during the pre-trial stage as well as those governing the conduct of the trial itself. Cultural factors, on the other hand, relate to the attitudes and expectations influencing the behaviour of those who participate in the criminal process, whether they be judges, public prosecutors, defendants or defence lawyers.

Coming to structural factors first, criminal justice in the Netherlands operates along the lines of the civil law tradition. Its basic features are inherited from the Napoleonic codes, introduced in the Netherlands by Napoleon at the beginning of the nineteenth century and subsequently replaced by national codes. In other words, unlike England and Wales, the Netherlands has an inquisitorial system of justice. Although one has always to be aware of the dangers involved in labelling national systems of justice adversarial or inquisitorial, one may agree with Mirjan Damaška that the core meaning of the opposition remains relatively certain:

> The adversarial mode of proceedings takes its shape from a contest or a dispute: it unfolds as an engagement of two adversaries before a relatively passive decision maker whose principal duty is to reach a verdict. The non-adversarial mode is structured as an official inquiry. Under the first system, the two adversaries take charge of most of procedural action, under the second, officials perform most activities.[5]

4 Compare B. Swart and J. Young, 'The European Convention on Human Rights and Criminal Justice in the Netherlands and the United Kingdom', in Fennell, id., p. 57.
5 M. Damaška, *The Faces of Justice and State Authority, A Comparative Approach to the Legal Process* (1986) 3.

42

One may add that inquisitorial systems are based on the belief that the state is best equipped to carry out an objective investigation into the truth, since parties to the proceedings might have an interest in concealing it. As other scholars have written recently:

> The legitimacy of the inquisitorial procedure in a democratic context requires an inordinate amount of faith in the integrity of the state and its capacity to pursue truth unprompted by partisan pressures of individual self-interest and untrammelled by equality of arms.[6]

It is obvious, therefore, that the very premises upon which inquisitorial systems are built make these systems more vulnerable to criticism from a human-rights perspective than adversarial systems, whatever difficulties adversarial systems may encounter in securing a fair trial to the accused.

While structural factors did not favour a strong rights culture within the context of criminal proceedings in the Netherlands, the same could be said of cultural factors. It has always been a typical characteristic of Dutch society as a whole that it attaches high value to avoiding conflicts, reaching compromises, and building consensus. In this tradition, the primary goal of law and politics is to keep society together and to create a measure of harmony between its members. Relatively low value is, therefore, attached to fighting out conflicts at the point of the sword, since this might jeopardize societal peace. To provide but one illustration, Dutch criminal law does not only forbid offending groups on account of their race, but also on the grounds of their religion, sex or sexual preference. The rules of criminal procedure and the use that is being made of them reflect these general inclinations. For a long time, criminal justice in the Netherlands too was marked by its inclination to avoid conflicts. Other characteristics used to be its paternalism and its mildness. To quote Antonie Peters, 'virtually undisputed confidence' was placed 'in the judicial wisdom of magistrates on whom wide discretionary powers could therefore be conferred'.[7] The mildness of criminal justice in the Netherlands is linked with its paternalism. It had to do with the tendency of the courts to see those who had committed criminal offences as members of a family who should be reintegrated rather than punished. However beneficial these features may often have been to the individual accused, they did not contribute to placing a high value on his or her individual rights.

The traditional features mentioned here apply to criminal justice in the Netherlands as it used to function at the time the European Convention was ratified. They relate to a society that was relatively closed and at peace with itself, in which social cohesion was strong and the crime rate low. Since then, a process of change has set in. These familiar cultural characteristics are

---

6 N. Jörg et al., 'Are Inquisitorial and Adversarial Systems Converging?' in Fennell et al., op. cit., n. 3, pp. 41, 43.
7 A. Peters, 'Main Currents in Criminal Law Theory' in *Criminal Law in Action*, eds. J. van Dijk et al. (1986) at 25.

43

disappearing slowly but, so it seems, inexorably. Explanations are not hard to find. Economic growth, industrialization, internationalization, cultural changes, immigration, the growth of crime rates, and the rise of new forms of criminality are but some of the many causes that have brought about fundamental changes in society and, with it, in its criminal justice system. In their turn, these changes have created a new need for protecting the rights of the suspect and the accused in the criminal process.

The impact of the European Convention and of other human rights treaties on criminal procedure in the Netherlands coincides in time with the deep social transformations that have occurred over the forty-five years since the Convention was ratified. In a way, the impact of human rights instruments may be looked at as a part of a larger process. To a considerable extent, the European Convention and other treaties provide compensation for the loss of traditional values. For instance, to the extent that the relative mildness of criminal justice in the Netherlands is gradually becoming a thing of the past, the accused has more reasons to cling to his or her rights. On the other hand, human rights treaties offer new answers to new and hitherto unknown problems. To describe their impact on criminal justice in the Netherlands without any reference to a larger societal context would amount to ignoring the main reasons why the European Convention now exerts such an enormous influence on the administration of criminal justice.

TRANSFORMATIONS

As has been remarked already, civil law systems of justice have their own problems with securing a fair trial for the accused, which may be different from the problems encountered by common law systems. Consequently, some of the problems that I will discuss below do not exist in the United Kingdom, or not to the same degree. Moreover, one should also be aware of the fact that there is considerable variation among civil law systems themselves. The difficulties encountered by the Netherlands are not always the same as those in, for instance, Germany or France. In other words, parts of my account are concerned with circumstances that are unique to the Netherlands.

In discussing developments in the Netherlands, I shall first turn my attention to four different specific problem areas: trials in the absence of the accused, the examination of witnesses and the use of hearsay evidence, delays in conducting criminal trials, and interrogation of suspects by the police. I shall then turn to the European Convention as a general incentive for improving the quality of criminal justice and making it more rights-oriented. Finally, I shall discuss a number of side-effects of the influence exerted by the Convention.

44

© Blackwell Publishers Ltd 1999

1. *Trial in the absence of the accused*

In the Dutch legal system, a trial in the absence of the accused is not categorically ruled out. In actual practice, such trials frequently occur. In particular, foreign accused and accused whose abode is not known to the authorities are regularly tried in their absence. The adverse consequences of this system to the accused are softened by providing them with a remedy. In most cases this remedy consists of an appeal to a court of appeal, which will then conduct a new trial or, in the words of the European Court in the case of *Colozza* v. *Italy*, proceed to a 'fresh determination of the charge'.[8] However, the accused may not show up for these proceedings either. As a matter of principle, the accused does so at his or her own risk, no trial *de novo* being possible after the court of appeal has decided the case.

Ever since the European Court of Human Rights first pronounced on trials in the absence of the accused in the case of *Colozza* v. *Italy*, and even before, the admissibility of trials *in absentia* had been the subject of much legal controversy in the Netherlands, and the European Convention played a crucial part in the debate. It is fair to say that trials in the absence of the accused are now less readily accepted than used to be the case twenty or even ten years ago.

One particular aspect of the problem used to be that lawyers who wanted to defend their absent clients in court were, as a matter of principle, not permitted to do so even if their clients had given them their consent. Under the influence of the European Convention, the Dutch Supreme Court started to make exceptions to this traditional rule during the 1980s and 1990s. But there remained many situations in which defence lawyers were not permitted to act on behalf of their absent clients. The decisions of the European Court of 1994 in the cases of *Lala* and *Pelladoah* v. *The Netherlands* put an end to this practice.[9] The Court considered the existing restrictions to be incompatible with the right of every accused to be defended by counsel.

Meanwhile, to permit a defence lawyer to defend his or her absent client is a satisfactory solution only in a situation in which lawyer and client are in touch with one another and have been able to discuss the client's case. The situation is very different when no one is able to tell whether or not the accused is aware of the date of the trial, not even the defence lawyer who has been appointed *ex officio* to defend the accused. In line with the European Court's case law requiring that the contracting states must exercise sufficient diligence in trying to serve a summons on the accused,[10] the Dutch courts have gradually required public prosecutors to make greater efforts to reach the accused, thus reducing appreciably the number of trials *in absentia*. On

---

8 ECHR 12 February 1985, Series A 89.
9 ECHR 22 September 1994, Series A 297-A *(Lala)*, and 22 September 1994, Series A 297-B *(Pelladoah)*.
10 ECHR 28 August 1991, Series A 208-B (*F.C.B.* v. *Italy*), and ECHR 12 October 1992, Series A 245-C (*T.* v. *Italy*).

the other hand, these trials have certainly not died out. This is mainly explained by the fact that, according to established case law, the accused too must show diligence in being kept informed of the progress of a criminal case, notably by complying with the duty of every citizen to inform municipal authorities of any change of address. This requirement of diligence plays a special role where the accused has appealed against his or her conviction by a court of first instance, since the very fact that he or she has appealed implies an awareness of criminal proceedings pending. Meanwhile, whether or not Dutch case law has succeeded in striking a fair balance between the due diligence of public prosecutors in trying to serve a summons on the accused and the diligence expected of the accused is open to doubt.[11] It seems to me that trials *in absentia* are still too readily accepted.

2. *Examination of witnesses and the use of hearsay evidence*

Traditionally, civil law systems of justice have weaker inhibitions about the use of hearsay evidence than do common law systems of justice. This is particularly true for the Netherlands. In the (not so distant) past one of the most characteristic features of public trials in the Netherlands was the almost total absence of witnesses. Witnesses were interviewed during pre-trial investigations either by the police or by an investigating judge, or by both. Statements of witnesses made out of court could be used as evidence virtually without any limitation. This practice made it almost superfluous for public prosecutors to summon witnesses in court. On the other hand, to summon a witness was usually hardly more rewarding for the defence since the trial court always remained free to use out-of-court witness statements as evidence if it considered that statement to be more credible than a deposition in open court.

Nowhere has the European Convention effected such fundamental changes in national habits and philosophies prevailing in the Netherlands than in the field of hearing witnesses. It is not an exaggeration to speak of a small cultural revolution here. Although changes set in earlier, without any doubt the turning point in developments is the decision of the European Court of 1986 in the case of *Unterpertinger* v. *Austria*, the first case on the right of the accused to question witnesses to have been decided by the Court.[12] The Court made it clear that, as a rule, the statement of a witness cannot be used as evidence against the accused, unless the defence has been given an opportunity to question the witness. From then on, the right of the accused to summon and question witnesses became one of the most disputed issues in Dutch courts and, as the years went by, the appearance of witnesses in open court in cases in which the accused denied the charges

11 Compare the Report of the European Commission of Human Rights, 16 October 1996 in the case of *Menckeberg* v. *The Netherlands* (not yet reported).
12 ECHR 24 November 1986, Series A 110.

46

gradually became a frequent and normal occurrence. As courts, public prosecutors, and defence lawyers became more familiar with the appearance of witnesses, there was a growing awareness of the importance of putting witnesses (and experts) on the stand. Perhaps the Netherlands will soon reach the point where the appearance of witnesses is the rule, rather than the exception it used to be in the past. All this is highly beneficial to the quality of criminal justice in the Netherlands.

Nevertheless, important problems remain. One of the most controversial and thorny issues still is the protection of vulnerable witnesses. At the beginning of the 1980s, the Dutch Supreme Court accepted the practice of granting anonymity to witnesses who feared for their life or physical integrity, for the purpose of eliciting a statement from them. It permitted the use of these out-of-court statements as evidence against the accused, even in cases in which the defence had been given no, or hardly any, proper opportunity to question the witness, and it did not disapprove of convictions solely based on statements of anonymous persons. In 1989, in the case of *Kostovski* v. *The Netherlands*, the European Court struck a number of important blows against the practice that had developed in the Netherlands.[13] Among other things, the case led to new and elaborate legislation on the protection of witnesses. The 1993 Act on the protection of vulnerable witnesses does not completely rule out the use of anonymous statements, but it does restrict their use in a number of ways. Meanwhile, the European Court has reached a decision on two other complaints against the Netherlands. In *Doorson* v. *The Netherlands*, decided in 1996, it made clear that Article 6 of the European Convention does not forbid the use of statements of anonymous persons in all circumstances. A year later, in the case of *Van Mechelen and others* v. *The Netherlands*, it did not approve of the use of statements of anonymous police officers as evidence against the accused.[14]

Another situation in which the rights of the accused conflict with the interests of witnesses, giving rise to many discussions, is that of witnesses who might suffer physical or mental harm as a consequence of being obliged to appear in court and to testify in the presence of the accused. One may, for instance, think of victims of violent crimes and of sexual offences. In actual practice, courts often resort to balancing the interests of the accused against those of the witness in reaching a decision on whether the witness will have to appear or not. An important consideration in reaching a decision is whether or not the witness has already been questioned by an investigating judge in the presence of the accused's lawyer and whether that lawyer is able to convince the court that a number of questions still remain to be answered.

---

13 ECHR 20 November 1989, Series A 166. For an English-language analysis of its importance, see A. Beijer et al., 'Witness Evidence, Article 6 of the European Convention on Human Rights and the Principle of Open Justice' in Fennell et al., op. cit., n. 3, p. 283.
14 ECHR 26 March 1996, 23 EHRR 330 (1996), and 22 April 1997, 25 EHRR 647 (1997).

So far, complaints against this balancing of interests by Dutch courts has not been declared admissible in Strasbourg.[15]

3. Hearing within a reasonable time

In the Dutch legal system, reaching a final verdict in a criminal case can be extremely time-consuming. The reasons are partly of a structural nature and directly related to the system of appeals. In virtually all criminal cases, both the public prosecutor and the accused are entitled to appeal against the verdict of the court of first instance. Courts of appeal will then proceed to a fresh determination of the charges. Against their decision, both the accused and, with some exceptions, the public prosecutor may appeal on points of law to the Supreme Court. It is obvious that this system does not make it easy to respect the accused's right to a speedy trial. In some respects, the European Convention has even added to the difficulties already existing. For instance, hearing witnesses more often in open court usually prolongs the time needed for reaching a decision in a criminal case.

From the point of view of numbers, complaints against protracted proceedings are easily at the top of all those raised in Dutch courtrooms on the grounds of non-compliance with European Convention. My personal guesstimate is that this is raised in one out of ten cases and accepted by the courts in one out of twenty. In less serious cases, courts will normally provide compensation for a breach of Article 6 of the Convention by reducing the sentence imposed. In more serious ones they will dismiss the case altogether. In such unforeseen ways the Convention somehow contributes to the preservation of a relatively mild sentencing climate.

As a matter of course, courts will follow Strasbourg case law in deciding whether or not the Convention has been violated. However, Dutch case law has become considerably more detailed; the case law of the Supreme Court alone amounts to almost two hundred reported cases over the past twenty years. Nevertheless, in 1992, and again in 1993, the European Court criticized the Netherlands for not applying the proper criteria in assessing whether certain delays amount to a breach of Article 6.[16]

4. Police interrogations

In the Netherlands, all suspects and accused have the right to remain silent. They must be informed of that right before they are questioned. Moreover, the law forbids putting any undue pressure on the suspect and the accused; they must remain free not to answer questions. A failure by the authorities

15 Compare, for example, European Commission 17 March 1995 and Committee of Ministers 15 May 1996 in *Finkensieper* v. *The Netherlands*, 39 *Yearbook of the European Convention on Human Rights* (1996) 374.
16 ECHR 25 November 1992, Series A 248-A (*Abdoella* v. *The Netherlands*) and 26 May 1993, Series A 248-B (*Bunkate* v. *The Netherlands*).

48

to respect these principles will lead to the statements obtained being excluded as evidence. During questioning, the suspect and the accused have a right to be assisted by a lawyer. There is only one exception, but a major one, to this right: police interrogations.

For some twenty years now, there has been a debate on the desirability of granting suspects the right to be assisted by a lawyer during police interrogations. In 1983, the Supreme Court held that, under Dutch law, suspects enjoy no general right to be assisted by a lawyer during police interrogation.[17] In that decision, no reference was made to the European Convention. Recently, the Supreme Court held that such a right cannot be derived from Article 6 of the European Convention.[18] Apparently, in its view the judgment of the European Court in the case of *Murray* v. *United Kingdom* does not have any particular consequences for police interrogations in the Netherlands – a debatable assumption.[19] In actual practice, some police forces admit lawyers as a matter of course while others are still strongly opposed to the idea. Unfortunately, while police interrogation practices have become more controversial over the years, there is, as yet, no parliamentary majority in favour of granting suspects the right to be assisted by counsel during questioning.

Another safeguard, sometimes presented as an attractive alternative to the presence of counsel, has a better chance of being accepted in the near future: the recording or videotaping of police interrogations. In 1998, the Public Prosecutions Department declared that, as a matter of principle, it did not object to this safeguard being introduced. However, 'practical considerations' led it to propose that the recording or taping of interrogations be limited to offences carrying a maximum prison sentence of twelve years or more. In a reaction to this proposal the Minister of Justice stated that the line should be drawn at eight years. Even so, in the vast majority of criminal cases interrogations would still not have to be recorded or taped.

5. The European Convention as a general incentive

In this section, I have given four examples of how the European Convention has, to a greater or lesser extent, exerted an influence on developments in the field of criminal justice and how it contributed to making criminal proceedings in the Netherlands more 'adversarial' and more rights-oriented. Other examples could be given. It is, for instance, unlikely that Dutch courts would, at the end of the 1970s, have adopted the rule that illegally obtained evidence must be excluded, if the Netherlands had not become a party to the European Convention. In a more general sense, one could say that the Convention has

17 SC 22 November 1983, NJ 1984, 805.
18 SC 13 May 1997, NJ 1998, 152.
19 ECHR 8 February 1996, 22 EHRR 29–75 (1996).

49

been important in two different ways. On the one hand, it has contributed to heightening standards where the reliability of evidence is concerned. On the other hand, it has been influential in creating a sharper awareness of the need to keep the police and other authorities in check in conducting their investigations and to subject their activities to close judicial scrutiny.

Undoubtedly, as a result of criminal proceedings having become more 'adversarial', the quality of criminal justice has considerably increased, in that the truth-finding process yields more reliable results. To reduce the numbers of trials *in absentia*, to put witnesses on the stand far more often, and to strengthen adversarial elements in proceedings in other ways are all incentives for the courts to assess the available evidence more thoroughly and more carefully before reaching a verdict. In a way, one could also say that the Convention obliges, or at least invites, national authorities to make use of the most reliable methods of collecting evidence available. This, at any rate, is an argument frequently advanced by the defence in criminal cases, for instance, with regard to line-ups or other identification methods. A few years ago, the importance of making systematic use of the insights of behavioural and other sciences was strongly underlined by three scholars in a book which, by analysing a number of recent criminal cases, held up an unflattering mirror to the face of all those involved in criminal justice.[20] Although their book can be criticized in a number of respects, the authors' main point is a valid one. It is still true that, in the Netherlands, insufficient use is being made of scientific proof and that, in this respect, the Netherlands lags behind a number of common law systems of justice.

Without any doubt too, in the past four decades the European Convention has become a touchstone in all public discussions on the eternal question of how to strike a fair balance between, on the one hand, the powers of the police and other authorities to conduct investigations and the rights of the accused and of third persons, on the other. A typical development of the 1990s, in which the Convention plays an important part, is the increased attention that is being paid to police investigation methods, whether old or of recent origin, during proactive investigations, such as the use of undercover agents, discreet surveillance, controlled deliveries.[21] Dissatisfaction with the use of these methods and unease over the secrecy surrounding them led to a parliamentary inquiry. In 1996, a parliamentary committee published a thirteen-volume report on a panoply of investigation methods, in which it laid bare the existing chaos, the lack of a firm basis in the law for many methods, and the virtual absence of effective political and judicial supervision.[22] A year later, the government responded by submitting a Bill to Parliament aimed at introducing new statutory provisions on proactive

---

20 An abridged version of their book has been published in English. See W. Wagenaar et al., *Anchored Narratives, The Psychology of Criminal Evidence* (1993).
21 Compare C. Brants and S. Field, *Participation Rights and Proactive Policing, Convergence and Drift in European Criminal Process* (1995).
22 *Inzake opsporing, Rapport van de Enquêtecommissie Opsporingsmethoden* (1996).

50

investigations in the Code of Criminal Procedure. Meanwhile, police investigation methods have become one of the most controversial and hotly contested issues in the courts. There is now hardly any major criminal case without protracted discussions on them.

6. Side-effects

Recent changes effected by the European Convention in the way criminal trials are being conducted in the Netherlands raise at least two fundamental concomitant issues. The one relates to the system of appeals, the other to the role of the judge.

The Dutch legal system, as well as many other civil law systems of justice, offers two opportunities for the public prosecutor as well as the accused to have the merits of a criminal case tried by a court: the proceedings at first instance, and the appeal proceedings. Proceedings on appeal imply that a court of appeal proceeds to a fresh determination of the charges, to a trial *de novo*. In theory, both the proceedings at first instance and the appeal proceedings must comply fully with all the requirements of a fair trial enshrined in human rights conventions. As I have noted earlier, under the influence of the European Convention criminal trials have become more 'adversarial' and, therefore, more complicated. They have also become more time-consuming and more costly. The question now is how long a system of two factual instances can still be maintained, given its rapidly increasing costs in terms of time and personnel. The strains put on the criminal justice system are becoming more visible every day. Will this system eventually have to be abolished, whether totally or partially? And would the accused suffer or benefit from such changes? In actual practice, one may already note a certain shift of emphasis towards the appeal courts. In more complicated criminal cases, there is an increasing tendency among defence lawyers and, to a lesser degree, public prosecutors to hurry through proceedings at first instance and to concentrate on proceedings before a court of appeal in which to conduct the real battle.

In an inquisitorial system of justice like that of the Netherlands, the role of the judge is not to act as a referee between the parties. Traditionally, it is his or her duty actively to carry out an investigation into the merits of a criminal case, with the public prosecutor and the defence lawyers acting more as associates or assistants in the endeavour than as opponents. In advance of the trial a judge will have studied the *dossier* carefully and will have developed some provisional thoughts on how to handle the case and on the points and issues that he or she would like clarified during the public hearing. During the trial the judge is firmly in charge. He or she may, for instance, decide that witnesses be heard without any request of the public prosecutor or the defence to that effect. However, as trials tend to become more adversarial than they were in the past, does this development not require judges to become more passive and to relinquish the primary

51

responsibility for the conduct of a trial to the public prosecutor and the defence? In other words, to behave more like judges in a common law system of justice? Obviously, the question touches on the very structure of criminal proceedings in inquisitorial systems. For the moment, however, I see few signs of such a development occurring, although it is true that judges become increasingly aware of what one may call a role-conflict.

EVALUATION

In the past four decades, criminal justice in the Netherlands has experienced profound transformations. The European Convention has broken through its traditional national isolation and has exposed it to new and unfamiliar concepts and ideas. The Convention has opened up the Dutch system to the world and forced it to adapt itself to international standards of fairness. In a way, one could say that the Dutch system of criminal justice has become less naïve, more sophisticated and more mature. One can only hope that this system, while gradually losing some of its traditional features and becoming more akin to other national systems in Europe, will succeed in preserving what one may consider to be its main positive characteristics – a tolerant attitude towards social deviance, a genuine care for individual offenders, and a mild penal climate.

The transformations that have been discussed have brought about a measure of convergence with common law systems of justice. By forcing inquisitorial systems of justice to become more adversarial, the European Convention acts, to some extent, as a motor of convergence between accusatorial and inquisitorial systems where their conceptions of a fair trial are concerned. However, this does not imply that a public hearing in the Netherlands now closely resembles a public hearing in a common law system of justice. Let me point to just two aspects of a public trial which show how strong the inquisitorial tradition still is in the Netherlands. First, during the hearing most of the questioning of witnesses and experts is still done by judges, who remain firmly in charge and carry out their own investigation into the merits of the case at hand. Secondly, there are still few objections against using a pre-trial statement of a witness as evidence if the court, after having heard the witness, is convinced that the pre-trial statement comes closer to the truth. More generally, while human rights treaties offer important stimuli for civil law systems to become more adversarial, the question is still open whether or not they make it necessary for these systems to relinquish inquisitorial habits and traditions completely. So far, the case law of the European Court does not seem to require this.[23] To quote Heike Jung, the main importance of the European Convention lies in the fact that it

23 Compare W.E. Haak, *'Welk type strafproces ligt ten grondslag aan het EVRM en aan de rechtspraak van het EHRM?'* (1996) 26 *Delikt en Delinkwent* 978.

permanently draws our attention to the existence of 'such meta-principles as fairness, checks and balances, predictability and procedural transparency'.[24]

In Europe, and the Netherlands in particular, debates on the right to a fair trial mainly take the European Convention as the commonly shared frame of reference. It is fair to say that the European view of what amounts to a fair trial is shaped by that convention, as interpreted and applied by the European Court of Human Rights. It is important to add here that the case law of the Court predominantly reflects the civil law conception of a fair trial. This is not surprising. Most of the states parties to the Convention have civil law systems of justice and most of the members of the Court come from those systems. However, the almost exclusive attention paid to the European Convention should not blind us to the fact that there are other international arenas in which the adversarial model of common law systems and the inquisitorial model of civil law systems compete with one another. Striking examples are provided by the two *ad hoc* international criminal tribunals recently created by the Security Council of the United Nations and by the statute of an international criminal court adopted in Rome in 1998. The statutes of both *ad hoc* courts and the rules of procedure adopted by them basically embrace the adversarial model; there is but little in them that reminds one of the inquisitorial model.[25] The same is true for the statute of the permanent international criminal court. Again, the explanation is not hard to find. For common law countries, the United States of America in particular, to adopt the inquisitorial model would be simply unacceptable while the reverse is apparently not the case for civil law countries. From this, I would conclude that, in the world at large, the adversarial model is politically and ideologically superior to the inquisitorial model. It is, therefore, likely that civil law systems like that of the Netherlands will, in the coming years, be confronted with the adversarial model and be influenced by it in new ways.

24 H. Jung, 'Criminal Justice – a European Perspective' [1993] *Crim. Law Rev.* 241.
25 Compare, also, the approach of the Yugoslavia Tribunal in its decision of 10 August 1995, case no. IT-94-J-T (*Public Prosecutor* v. *Tadic*) to the protection of witnesses with the approach taken by the European Court in the cases of *Doorson* and *Van Mechelen* and others.

JOURNAL OF LAW AND SOCIETY
VOLUME 26, NUMBER 1, MARCH 1999
ISSN: 0263-323X, pp. 54-71

Theory Meets Practice: Some Current Human Rights Challenges in Canada

JOHN HUCKER*

The article examines three recent situations in which human rights issues have been in the forefront of public policy debates in Canada. In the first, freedom of expression may have been compromised as a result of foreign policy considerations. The second case involves the sometimes contentious issue of equal pay for work of equal value. Thirdly, a current initiative aimed at resolving a longstanding claim by Aboriginal Canadians is examined in the context of principles of equality.

Canada has an impressive array of human rights instruments. A constitutionally entrenched Charter of Rights and Freedoms[1] sits at the summit, affirming basic political and civil rights. The Charter includes a strong equality clause[2] and is augmented by federal and provincial human rights codes which provide redress for the victims of discrimination. In deference to the country's changing cultural mosaic, a Canadian Multiculturalism Act[3] also encourages the preservation of diverse cultures. While not without their critics, Canadian courts have been broadly sympathetic to the objectives of the Charter and to the work of human rights agencies. The Charter has also been instrumental in sensitizing governments and the public to issues involving civil and political rights.[4] Economic and social rights present a

---

1 Canadian Charter of Rights and Freedoms, Part I of the Constitution Act, 1982, being schedule B the Canada Act 1982 (U.K.) 1982, c. 1.

2 id., s. 15(1).

3 S.C. 1988, c. 31.

4 In fact, the federal government provides funding through its Court Challenges Program for groups or individuals who wish to challenge laws or policies which they view as inconsistent with Charter guarantees, but who would otherwise be unable for financial reasons to pursue litigation. The programme is administered at arm's length from the government.

* *Secretary General, Canadian Human Rights Commission, 320 Queen Street, 15th Floor, Place de Ville, Tower 'A', Ottawa, Ontario K1A 1E1, Canada*

The ideas expressed herein should not be taken to represent the position of the Canadian Human Rights Commission. The author wishes to thank Ms. Jocelyne Cantin and Ms. Grace Brown for their assistance.

more difficult challenge. Although they feature in international instruments to which Canada is a party, they are not readily justiciable and efforts to give them substance and content at the domestic level tend to founder on the twin rocks of federal-provincial jealousies and the current disinclination to view the state as an appropriate agent for advancing social change.

In earlier articles[5] I have described some major features of Canada's human rights machinery. In the present paper I wish both to narrow and broaden the focus. The paper will be limited to a discussion of three recent examples where Canada's institutions have grappled with issues involving claims which fall within the broad rubric of human rights. While limited in number, the situations to be examined are varied in their subject matter and in the nature of the choices that confront decision makers. Collectively they suggest an ambivalence in Canada over the extent to which human rights principles should, in the final analysis, influence outcomes. The first case involves a current dispute over the constitutionally protected right to freedom of expression; the second concerns a recent, much publicized equality rights decision; the third example discusses a significant agreement recently concluded between the federal government and the Nisga'a aboriginal nation that attempts to find an appropriate balance between the rights of aboriginal Canadians and those of non-natives.

I. THE APEC CASE: HUMAN RIGHTS AT HOME AND ABROAD

Since the current federal government came to power in 1993, it has trodden an uneasy path between its desire to be seen to be advancing human rights internationally while at the same time seeking to increase Canada's links with nations in Asia and Latin America whose human rights records are less than stellar. By contrast to its neighbour to the south, Canada has generally favoured a policy of 'constructive engagement', believing that there is more to be gained from dialogue and diplomacy than from the condemnation of authoritarian regimes. This approach has not found universal favour, and Prime Minister Jean Chrétien encountered considerable criticism at home when he led high profile federal-provincial trade delegations to China and Indonesia while remaining silent about well documented human rights abuses in those countries.

The human rights versus business-as-usual debate has continued. However, the rights side of the equation appeared to gain ground in 1996 with the naming of a new Minister for Foreign Affairs. In a speech in February of the same year, the new Minister, Lloyd Axworthy, emphasized that henceforth Canada would take a leadership role on human rights at the United Nations and would emphasize 'Canadian values' in its relations

---

5 See J. Hucker, 'Towards Equal Opportunity in Canada: New Approaches, Mixed Results' (1995) 26 *St-Mary's Law J.* 841; J. Hucker, 'Anti-discrimination Laws in Canada: Human Rights Commissions and the Search for Equality' (1997) 19 *Human Rights Q.* 547.

with other countries.[6] He subsequently took forceful positions on such issues as child labour[7] and the elimination of anti-personnel land mines.[8]

The Asia-Pacific Economic Cooperation forum (APEC), of which Canada was a founding member, was established in 1989 with the objective of increasing economic links in this fast-expanding region of the world. The organization holds an annual meeting which is customarily attended by heads of government and senior ministers. In November 1997, Canada as the rotating chair, hosted the APEC summit in Vancouver, British Columbia. During the period leading up to the meeting and throughout the two day event, considerable public protest was directed at the attendance of Indonesia's then-president Suharto. In addition to the bloody annexation of East Timor, Suharto's record of quashing dissenting voices was well known, and his government had been accused of widespread abuses including torture, imprisonment without trial, and the executions of political prisoners.

During the APEC meetings, students activists opposed to the presence of Suharto and the actions of his government in Indonesia organized demonstrations at the University of British Columbia (UBC), which was located close to the meeting site. Apparently motivated by security concerns, the Royal Canadian Mounted Police (RCMP) at one point used pepper spray to disperse demonstrators who were blocking a route shortly to be used by the APEC participants. The police also pulled down anti-Suharto and pro-free speech signs, and are alleged to have assaulted and strip searched some protestors. It is now known, that several months before the summit, Canada's Foreign Affairs Minister apologized to his Indonesian counterpart for anti-Suharto posters that had already begun to appear in Canadian cities.[9] In response to warnings from the Indonesian government that Suharto would not attend the Asia-Pacific summit meeting if embarrassed

6 'Axworthy vows to take stand on rights' *Globe and Mail (Toronto)*, 14 February 1996, A-7A.
7 A study funded by the federal government concluded that the idea of labelling carpets imported to Canada as 'made without child labour' would do little to help exploited children in the developing world. See 'Carpet labelling not worth the expense, report says' *Ottawa Citizen*, 3 October 1996, A4. See, further, 'Why the Third World needs child labour' *Globe and Mail (Toronto)*, 25 February 1997, A 21: 'The Canadian stance on child labour comes almost entirely in terms of Canadian perceptions and interests . . . with little regard for social conditions, economic organizations and cultural mores of foreign countries'.
8 Canada, along with the Foreign Ministers from Austria, Norway, and South Africa, took the lead role in developing and seeking support for a global agreement to ban anti-personnel land mines. Canada hosted the Land Mines Conference held in Ottawa, in December 1997, at which time 122 countries signed the Convention on the Prohibition of the Use, Stockpiling, Production and Transfer of Anti-Personnel Mines and on their Destruction, which has become known as the Ottawa Convention. See, 'Axworthy hopes agreement to rid world of untended weapons can be in place by 2000' *Globe and Mail (Toronto)*, 3 October 1996 and 'Mine treaty signed into law' *Ottawa Citizen*, 17 September 1998, C1.
9 See 'Just how far should police go in protecting dictators?' *Vancouver Sun*, 10 September 1998, A15. The poster campaign led by the East Timor Alert Network protested Suharto's occupation of East Timor and the plight of ethnic Chinese in Indonesia.

56

by demonstrators, the Canadian government gave assurances that protestors would be kept away from the Indonesian president.

Following the UBC campus demonstrations, approximately fifty individual complaints were lodged with the RCMP Public Complaints Commission[10] by protestors, some of whom were among those pepper-sprayed and arrested. The complaints alleged that the conduct of the RCMP, violated the protestors' constitutional right to freedom of speech and expression. On February 20, 1998, the Chairman of the Public Complaints Commission announced that an inquiry would be held into all matters relating to the complaints.[11] Specifically, the inquiry would address:

> Whether the conduct of members of the RCMP involved in the events that took place during, or in conjunction with demonstrations during the APEC conference were appropriate in the circumstances;
> Whether the conduct of the members of the RCMP involved in the events was consistent with respect for the fundamental freedoms guaranteed by section 2 of the Canadian Charter of Rights and Freedom.[12]

Events preceding and, in particular, subsequent to the APEC imbroglio have given rise to a number of questions. First, of course there is the apparent inconsistency in Canada's human rights stance, evidenced by a readiness to provide assurances to a dictator that he would not have to face protests in Vancouver, even if this required giving short shrift to the constitutional rights of Canadian protestors. The irony is underlined by the fact that only a few months after the Canadian government went to great lengths to shield President Suharto from protest Canadian style, he was driven from office as a result of rather more serious demonstrations in Jakarta led by Indonesian students.[13]

APEC has also provided continuing grist for the political mill. One of the major issues to have emerged concerns the role of the Prime Minister's office *vis-à-vis* the police. There is some evidence that the Prime Minister's staff were active in directing the RCMP to remove demonstrators and that they were motivated more by a desire to avoid political embarrassment than by fear for the security of visiting government leaders. If found to be the case,

10 The Public Complaints Commission, established in March 1986, is an independent administrative tribunal empowered to conduct external and independent reviews of public complaints concerning the conduct of members of the RCMP in the course of their duties. Royal Canadian Mounted Police Act R.S.C. 1985, ch. R-10.

11 The public hearings were to commence on 5 October 1998. See 'Why APEC allegations are so serious' *Globe and Mail (Toronto)*, 5 October 1998, A23.

12 Section 2 of the Charter (above, n. 1) provides that
'Everyone has the following fundamental freedoms:
Freedom of conscience and religion;
Freedom of thought, belief, opinion and expression;
Freedom of peaceful assembly;
Freedom of association.'

13 See 'The right to speak, the duty to speak' *Globe and Mail (Toronto)*, 22 September 1998, A30, and 'Will we finally put human rights before trade?' *Edmonton Journal*, 3 October 1998, F3.

57

this of course has serious implications for the democratic principle requiring a separation between the political apparatus and law enforcement agencies. The Prime Minister added further fuel to what was becoming something of a political firestorm by some insensitive remarks conveying a clear impression that he viewed the issues arising out of the APEC summit as trivial.[14]

Meanwhile, the planned hearing by the RCMP Public Complaint Commission ran into its own difficulties. These started with a dispute over the right of student complainants to be represented by counsel paid for by the federal government. The refusal of this request prompted a walkout by some lawyers, whose involvement had initially been on a *pro bono* basis.[15] The independence of the Commission and its capacity to deal fully and objectively with what rapidly became a political *cause célèbre* also became an issue as Parliament witnessed sustained attacks on the Solicitor General, who was the Minister with overall responsibility for the RCMP and the Public Complaints Commission. Parliamentary and press attacks gained in intensity when an opposition MP reported that he had overheard the Minister discussing the APEC hearings in a dismissive fashion while the two were fellow passengers on a flight.[16]

At the same time as these events were being played out, a contentious sub-plot developed, involving the fairness (or otherwise) of reporting of the APEC affair on CBC Television. The lead reporter was discovered to have been in regular e-mail contact with one of the main complainants, a law student, and to have encouraged the latter to pursue his case against what the reporter characterized as 'the forces of darkness' that is, the federal government.[17] A letter of complaint from a senior official in the Prime Minister's Office succeeded in having the reporter taken off the story but, perhaps not surprisingly, prompted redoubled charges of political interference. A further complication arose when the person appointed to chair the inquiry into the APEC complaints temporarily withdrew when an allegation was made that he had been overhead making remarks on the substance of the case while gambling at a casino. The hearing was suspended while the issue of possible bias was referred for adjudication by the Federal Court of Canada.[18]

---

14 On one occasion he jokingly referring to his own use of pepper as a table condiment, and in responding to opposition attacks in Parliament opined that in dealing with demonstrators pepper spray was preferable to the use of baseball bats. See 'Chrétien expresses regret for clash at APEC Summit' *Ottawa Citizen*, 23 September 1998, A3 and 'Pepper spray beats bats?' *Ottawa Citizen*, 20 October 1998, A9.

15 See 'Scott rejects legal funding for student protesters' *Vancouver Sun*, 17 October 1998, A1.

16 See 'Scott lying on APEC remarks: NDP' *Globe and Mail (Toronto)*, 7 October 1998, A2 and 'Scott denies compromising public inquiry into APEC' *Ottawa Citizen*, 7 October 1998, A2.

17 See 'Static from Ottawa interferes with CBC' *Toronto Star*, 14 November 1998, A2 and 'Memo to PM's media flunky: news is schmooze' *Toronto Star*, 14 November 1998, A2.

18 See 'APEC inquiry suspended as leader faces accusation' *Globe and Mail (Toronto)*, 24 October 1998, A1 and 'How not to take criticism' *Globe and Mail (Toronto)*, 30 October 1998, A24.

58

While the events surrounding the 1997 APEC summit meeting have sometimes taken on elements of comic opera, the underlying issues remain serious and substantive. At the international level, the government's efforts to balance trade with human rights have been inconsistent and have left it vulnerable to criticism.[19] Domestically, the final verdict on the alleged denial of a constitutionally protected right to freedom of speech and assembly which occurred in Vancouver may be some time in coming. Whether political imperatives overrode civil liberties in November 1997 remains an open question, although preliminary indications are that such was indeed the case. But caution is in order, since initial impressions have been largely conditioned by repeated TV showings of a middle aged police officer directing a jet of pepper spray at demonstrators at close quarters. The events that preceded this graphic image have yet to be brought out in any objective fashion.

II. PAY EQUITY: THE UNION VERSUS THE GOVERNMENT

In the summer of 1998 a federal human rights tribunal handed down its decision in a complaint which had been filed more than a decade earlier by the Public Service Alliance of Canada (PSAC) alleging that large numbers of federal public servants were the victims of discriminatory pay differentials. The basis of the complaint was that jobs that were predominantly occupied by women were underpaid by comparison to those of equal value where men predominated. The tribunal ordered the respondent, the federal Treasury Board, to eliminate the wage gap and provide wage adjustments retroactive to 8 March 1985.

Under normal circumstances all of this would probably have passed without great fanfare, since the concept of equal pay for work of equal value had been a feature of the Canadian Human Rights Act for more than twenty years.[20] The notion that a woman or man doing the same work for the same employer should receive equal compensation (equal pay for equal work) is

---

19 Prime Minister Chrétien adopted a more forceful human rights stand for the 1998 APEC summit, to be held in Malaysia. See 'PM pledges tough stand on human rights in Malaysia' *Toronto Star*, 11 November 1998, A7: 'The Prime Minister, who has long been bedeviled by the perception that he is soft on human rights if a tougher message would impede trade, said yesterday he will carry Canadian objections on Malaysia's treatment of former deputy prime minister and finance minister, Anwar Ibrahim'. See, also, 'Human Rights call met with hostility' *Financial Times*, 16 November 1998, 3: 'APEC's trade liberalisation agenda was further complicated over the weekend after Canada took a robust stance on human rights . . . The Canadian initiative produced a hostile response from their Malaysian hosts'.
20 All provinces except Alberta also have some form of pay equity legislation or policies in place, which provide for work and pay comparisons within the same establishment. Six provinces – Manitoba (1985); Ontario (1988), Prince Edward Island (1988); Nova Scotia (1988); New Brunswick (1989) and Quebec (1997) – have adopted a regulatory approach rather than a complaints-based model. All provinces include the public service; all except New Brunswick include the broader public sector; and Ontario and Quebec include private sector employers with ten or more employees.

a clear-cut example of the principle of non-discrimination. Its expansion to include situations where the jobs are not identical but the skill and effort involved are equivalent (equal pay for work of equal value, or pay equity) has, however, proven more problematic. In its fundamentals the concept of pay equity is not difficult to grasp. If, to take one example, a transportation company pays its drivers (preponderantly male) more than it pays its dispatchers (largely a female group), this probably reflects the importance historically placed on physical effort and attaches insufficient weight to administrative tasks, which are traditionally seen as 'women's work' and whose different set of skills are often undervalued.

Section 11 (1) of the Canadian Human Rights Act provides that 'it is a discriminatory practice for an employer to establish or maintain differences in wages between male and female employees employed in the same establishment who are performing work of equal value.' Since its enactment, s. 11 has led to the filing of a steady but unremarkable number of complaints. When brought by an individual or a small group of workers, a pay equity complaint can be dealt with relatively easily. An investigation is undertaken to assemble basic data on the tasks performed by the complainant. If, as is usually the case, the complainant is a woman and is working in a predominantly female job category, the investigator will seek to find a position or category of work in the same establishment[21] that is predominantly male. The duties of the respective jobs are then assessed according to four criteria prescribed by the Act: skill, effort, responsibility, and working conditions.[22] If the complainant's work is found to be underpaid, the employer will be required to make appropriate adjustments to its pay scales and to reimburse the complainant for wages foregone as a result of past undercompensation.

To this point pay equity can be viewed as a branch of more general anti-discrimination law, building on general equality principles if sometimes arcane in its application. But we enter a different realm if s. 11 is invoked not by a handful of underpaid individuals but by a trade union. Here, human rights laws become entangled in an array of issues revolving around labour relations, collective bargaining and, not least, cost. Employers are likely to resist any settlement proposals and will often raise legal challenges to the complaint. The result can be inordinate delay and resultant acrimony between the parties which frequently becomes a matter of public record via press or television reports.

---

21 The term 'establishment' is employed in s. 11. It is usually but not always synonymous with 'employer'. For an interesting discussion, see P. Hughes, The Evolution of a Concept: The Identity of 'Employer' For Pay Equity Purposes, (1994–95) 8 *Cdn. J. of Administrative Law and Practice* 159.

22 Canadian Human Rights Act, s. 11(2) reads: 'in assessing the value of work performed by employees employed in the same establishment, the criterion to be applied is the composite of the skill, effort and responsibility required in the performance of the work and the conditions under which the work is performed.'

Which brings us back to the case of *PSAC* v. *Treasury Board*.[23] This in fact involved two separate pay equity complaints. The first was filed in December 1984 on behalf of union members in the predominantly female clerical group whose pay was compared to that of the predominantly male programme administration group. The second was filed in March 1990 on behalf of six other female-predominant occupational groups and sought to use as comparators all other male-predominant groups in the federal public service. Estimates of the exact number of individual employees who stood to benefit from the case range from 50,000 to as many as 200,000.[24]

After the initial PSAC complaint was laid, the employer and the union established a 'joint initiative' to determine the extent of any wage gap contrary to s. 11. This led to an extensive exercise involving the development of a gender-neutral job evaluation plan followed by a series of job evaluations across much of the public service. The ill-fated initiative, which continued for some five years and was characterized by growing mistrust between the parties, ended in failure in 1990, at which time the Treasury Board announced that it was making a payment of $1.3 billion which according to its own calculations was sufficient to bridge any wage gap.[25] Subsequent to the Board's unilateral effort to resolve matters, PSAC filed its second, omnibus complaint. The Commission referred both complaints for a hearing before the Canadian Human Rights Tribunal in 1991. After withstanding procedural challenges from the employer, the tribunal panel proceeded to deliver an initial decision in January 1996[26] holding that the results of the joint initiative were reliable and could form the basis for legal arguments from the parties directed to the appropriate methodology for calculating and correcting wage inequities in accordance with s. 11 of the Act.[27]

After a total of more than 250 days, which made it the longest-running human rights hearing in Canadian history, the tribunal found in favour of PSAC. No specific award for lost wages was included, rather, the union and the employer were given a period of one year to agree upon the distribution

23 Decision of the Canadian Human Rights Tribunal, Phase II, 29 July 1998 (unreported).
24 The final figure will depend upon payroll records maintained by the Treasury Board as the employer for the federal public service. The wide variation is attributable in part to uncertainty over how many past employees, including temporary workers, are found to have worked for the government during the relevant period.
25 President of Treasury Board announced equalization adjustments for various predominantly female groups to bring their wages into line with those of predominantly male groups performing work of equal value, 26 January 1990. The union proclaimed that the Treasury Board had not respected its commitment to the implementation of pay equity following the study. See 'Issues in Human Rights – Equal Pay' in *CHRC Annual Report 1990* (1990) 48; and 'Issues in Human Rights – Pay Equity' in *CHRC Annual Report 1991* (1991) 56.
26 *PSAC* v. *Canada (Treasury Board)* (no. 2) (1996) 29 C.H.R.R. D/349.
27 An important subsidiary issue before the tribunal involved the effects of s. 14 of the Commission's Equal Wages Guidelines which reads, 'Where a comparison is made between the occupational group that filed a complaint alleging a difference in wages and other occupational groups, those occupational groups are deemed to be one group.'

61

of the moneys due, which were to be calculated in accordance with a methodology proposed by the Canadian Human Rights Commission during the hearing. In perhaps the most significant element of its decision, the tribunal ruled that lost wages should be awarded from March 1985, the date when the parties had announced their joint initiative, and were to include interest calculated from the same date. The thirteen year retroactivity period, combined with the payment of interest, will have the effect of more than doubling the amount of any final award.

The PSAC decision received extensive media coverage, primarily because of the potential scale of the award. The absence of a quantum in the tribunal's lengthy decision did not discourage speculation, and figures into the billions of dollars were mentioned, with an estimate of $5 billion being the sum most frequently quoted.[28] All of this led to some highly charged exchanges between, on one side, the union and its supporters who called on the government to meet its obligations under the law without further delay and, on the other, editorialists and diverse pundits who expressed emotions ranging from distress to outrage at the thought of handing over such an enormous slice of the taxpayers' money to a group of civil servants. Positions hardened further when the government announced that it intended to seek judicial review of the tribunal's decision,[29] thereby guaranteeing that the drama would continue to play out for further months and possibly years.

PSAC v. *Treasury Board* is of interest on a number of levels. First, of course, it throws into sharp relief the dilemma which can result from the implementation of equality rights law in a setting and on a scale which has significant financial consequences for an employer. It is hard to imagine that the Liberal government which enacted the Canadian Human Rights Act in 1977 could have foreseen that some twenty years later a successor would be

28 See, for example, 'The $5-billion snapshot' *Ottawa Citizen*, 4 October 1998, A6. The same article goes on to observe that 'three citizens took seven years to make a decision that would wipe out the federal surplus in one fell swoop'.

29 In announcing its decision to seek judicial review in the PSAC case, the government emphasized that it remained committed to the principles of pay equity but suggested that the tribunal in PSAC had misapplied the relevant law. In arguing that it was turning to the courts to seek clarification of the law, the government pointed to an earlier decision of the Federal Court in *Bell Canada* v. *Communications, Energy and Paperworkers Union, Canadian Telephone Employees Association and the Canadian Human Rights Commission* (Decision of Muldoon J., Federal Court of Canada, Trial Division, 17 March 1998). In the Bell Canada case, the judge had ruled *inter alia* that s. 11 of the Canadian Human Rights Act did not envisage comparisons between generic groupings of male-preponderant and female-preponderant jobs. In Muldoon J.'s words, 'this nouvelle vague is exactly what is not contemplated by section 11 of the Act. Section 11 contemplates discrimination as between specific comparators.' (Reasons for decision, at p. 21.). The decision in Bell is currently under appeal. If it is affirmed by the Federal Court of Appeal, the holding in the case will effectively preclude the use of pay equity complaints to attack more widespread instances of wage discrimination. It will simply not be possible to undertake the job-to-job, person-to-person comparisons envisaged by Muldoon J. when several hundred or even several thousand jobs are at issue, as was the case in the Bell and PSAC complaints.

62

directed to pay several billion dollars to its own employees as the result of a complaint filed under the same law. The discomfort of current Ministers in dealing with the fallout from the PSAC complaint has been palpable.[30]

Secondly, the decision illustrates some of the difficulties that can arise when there is no clear consensus in support of a human rights ruling. Pay equity is an important but lesser known component of equality law. Most Canadians remain understandably unfamiliar with the concept, confusing it with equal pay for equal work or with the laws on employment equity (Canada's version of affirmative action). Moreover, posited equivalencies between sometimes widely differing types of work are inherently open to challenge. This is especially the case when determinations are heavily dependent upon the testimony of job evaluation experts whose language can sometimes leave the lay person bemused.[31]

Thirdly, as noted earlier, pay equity is a field where human rights laws intersect most directly and uncomfortably with issues of labour relations and collective bargaining. Under federal law a union which is dissatisfied with progress at the bargaining table is free to file a complaint against the employer under s. 11 of the Canadian Human Rights Act.[32] During a time of downsizing and wage freezes a growing number of pay equity cases coming before the Commission emerge out of this background. Several consequences are likely to flow from such a sequence of events, not least a rapid deterioration in labour relations between the parties, and a level of resentment on the part of the employer which is likely to manifest itself in a lack of co-operation with any investigation. For its part, the Commission is left in the uneasy position of being required to devote scarce resources to investigating a human rights complaint which both parties may subsequently seek to have withdrawn should relations between them improve.

As of this time, it is unclear how and when *PSAC* v. *Treasury Board* will ultimately be resolved. The Commission continues to favour a negotiated settlement between the parties. The union views the tribunal's ruling as vindication and asserts the rights of its members to receive the full amounts due. Although the government has applied for judicial review of the tribunal decision, it professes its openness to resuming negotiations whenever the union shows a willingness to compromise on the total cost.

---

30 See 'Government fights equity ruling: Ministers cite unfair formula in appeal. Two visibly uncomfortable cabinet ministers yesterday paid lip service to the principle of pay equity but said the federal government must appeal a landmark $5 billion ruling for the sake of all Canadians.' *Ottawa Citizen*, 28 August 1998, A6.

31 In *PSAC* v. *Treasury Board*, many weeks of hearing were given over to the testimony of experts called by the CHRC and the union, and their extensive cross-examination by counsel for the Treasury Board.

32 This apparent freedom is under challenge by a major employer which has argued *inter alia* the issue of union bad faith before the Federal Court. See *Bell Canada*, op. cit., n. 29.

63

III. ABORIGINAL SELF GOVERNMENT: THE CASE OF
THE NISGA'A

The story of Canada's aboriginal peoples is one of historical dispersal and dispossession whose consequences are still being felt.[33] The Canadian Human Rights Commission has described their situation as a 'national tragedy' and the greatest human rights challenge facing the country,[34] and studies have consistently shown that native Canadians enjoy a standard of living far inferior to that of their non-native counterparts, that they compare unfavorably in terms of health and life expectancy and suffer from chronically high unemployment rates.[35]

Governments have attempted to address these problems through a variety of social programmes and in recent years have placed increased emphasis on devolving direct responsibility for programme management to native bands and regional councils.[36] The negotiation of native land claims has also been a priority but settlements have been hard to achieve for a number of reasons, including the large scale of many comprehensive claims, resistance by provincial governments to potential settlements which are viewed, rightly or wrongly, as having an adverse impact on local communities and businesses, and an earlier emphasis on maintaining a clear distinction between claims to land or resources and issues of native self government.

Today there are two basic categories of native claims. So-called specific claims arise from the alleged non-fulfilment of earlier treaties signed between the Crown and aboriginal nations in Canada or the failure of government to meet other specific commitments. The second and generally more far-reaching group are 'comprehensive' claims. These are based upon assertions of continuing aboriginal title or rights to areas of land and resources. In the words of the federal government:

> The primary purpose of comprehensive claims settlements is to conclude agreements with Aboriginal groups that will resolve the legal ambiguities associated with the common law concept of Aboriginal rights. The process is intended to result in agreement on the special

33 See O. Dickason, *Canada's First Nations: A History of Founding Peoples from Earliest Times* (1992).
34 See CHRC, op. cit. (1990), n. 25, p. 19.
35 See, for example, 'Canada's squalid secret: Life on native reserves' *Globe and Mail (Toronto)*, 12 October 1998, A1: 'Canada may top the United Nations list for the highest quality of life in the world, but a new government study shows what the ranking hides: Native Canadians living on reserves fall far down in the pack, ranking worse than countries such as Mexico and Thailand.' See, also, 'Three Countries Face Their Indians' *New York Times*, 15 December 1996, E3. See, also, Canadian Royal Commission on Aboriginal Peoples, Canadian Communications Group, vols. 1–5 (1996). A discussion of the economic and social disadvantage experienced by Canada's aboriginal peoples appears in vol. 3, *Gathering Strength*.
36 The effectiveness of government funded programs has been a subject of ongoing debate. See, for example, 'The money pit: an Indian band's story. Taxpayers pour billions of dollars into the Samson Cree Reserve. That's good for the well-connected few. But most people there live in abject poverty' *Globe and Mail (Toronto)*, 24 October 1998, A 1.

rights Aboriginal peoples will have in the future with respect to lands and resources. The objective is to negotiate modern treaties which provide clear, certain and long-lasting definition of rights to lands and resources. Negotiated comprehensive claims settlements provide for the exchange of undefined Aboriginal rights for a clearly defined package of rights and benefits codified in constitutionally protected settlement agreements.[37]

Comprehensive claims have been settled in Yukon and the Northwest Territories, where land and resources remain under federal domain and provincial involvement was therefore not a complicating factor. In 1975 successful negotiations were also completed on a major claim brought by the Cree and Inuit of Northern Quebec. A spur to the settlement was the desire of the Quebec government to move ahead with a project to construct a vast hydroelectric project at James Bay on lands traditionally claimed by the native groups, who had threatened legal action to halt construction if their claims were not addressed.

With the passage of time sometimes comes wisdom, and there is now a general acceptance in government circles that any solution to the seemingly intractable challenges of redefining an appropriate place for aboriginal peoples in the broader Canadian polity must start with recognition of the principle of aboriginal self-government. Given that most native Canadians still live on a total of some 600 reserves scattered across the country and have a very limited economic base, practical models of self-government are not easily fashioned

In this context, current efforts to settle the comprehensive claim of the Nisga'a nation, a group of aboriginal communities located in North-west British Columbia near the border with Alaska, are of great significance. Both federal and provincial levels of government are parties to the proposed agreement, which includes substantial elements of aboriginal self-government. In order to understand the implications of the Nisga's agreement, some historical background is necessary.[38]

1. *Early efforts by the Nisga'a*

In January 1887, sixteen years after British Columbia joined Confederation as a province, Nisga'a elders first sought agreement from the Crown to negotiate a treaty to establish the Nisga'a's land claim. Faced with continuing pressure from the Nisga'a, the federal and provincial governments agreed to appoint two representatives to travel to the north coast to hear the Nisga'a case. Neither the federal nor provincial representative considered the question of title or the closely related question of treaties. The message

---

37 Indian and Northern Affairs Canada, Federal Policy for the Settlement of Native Claims, Ottawa, 1998.
38 See P. Tennant, *Aboriginal peoples and Politics: the land question in British Columbia* (1990). This book presents a comprehensive account of the history of the land question in British Columbia, and provides insight into court decisions, government policies, and land claim developments.

65

remained that the Crown owned the land and that governments would continue to discharge their duty by setting apart land they deemed sufficient for Indian use. Despite this setback, the Nisga'a continued to organize and in 1890 established their first Land Committee, to begin the campaign for recognition of their territorial rights. The Committee's subsequent efforts included an unsuccessful 1913 petition to the Privy Council.

In 1955 the Committee re-established itself as the Nisga'a Tribal Council and in 1968 Frank Calder, President of the Council, initiated proceedings in the British Columbia Supreme Court seeking a judicial declaration that the Nisga'a's aboriginal rights had never been lawfully extinguished. In 1969, the British Columbia Supreme Court accepted the province's legal arguments that the Nisga'a held no title, and even if they had, such title would have been implicitly extinguished by land legislation passed before 1871. The same argument prevailed before the British Columbia Court of Appeal. However, the Supreme Court of Canada viewed matters differently, concluding that the Nisga'a had held title to their land when the colonial government came into existence in 1858.[39] Reverberations from the Calder decision were far-reaching, since henceforth aboriginal title had to be addressed as a reality rather than a romantic myth. The ruling was instrumental in prompting the federal government to develop a policy providing for the negotiation of unsettled aboriginal land claims across Canada, and settlement discussions with the Nisga'a began in 1976.

For a number of years provincial governments in British Columbia maintained their earlier policy of refusing to negotiate issues of aboriginal title, with the result that until 1990 negotiations were conducted on a bilateral basis between Canada and the Nisga'a. However, in that year the provincial government reversed the stance of its predecessors and took its seat at the negotiating table. The three parties concluded an agreement-in-principle in 1996, and after intensive negotiations a final agreement was initialled on 4 August 1998. The agreement will come into effect once it is ratified by the Nisga'a through a referendum and after it has been implemented through the enactment of legislation at the federal and provincial levels.

2. Main features of the Nisga'a final agreement[40]

The agreement sets aside approximately 2,000 square kilometres of the Nass River Valley in North-western British Columbia as Nisga'a lands. The Nisga'a will own surface and subsurface resources and are awarded a share of timber, salmon stocks, and other wildlife. The agreement also provides the Nisga'a with substantial financial compensation which is intended to support economic growth in the region and help to break the cycle of dependency on

39 *Calder* v. *British Columbia* (Attorney-General) (1973) SCR 313 34 D.L.R.(3D) 145; affirming 13 D.L.R. (3d) 64 (B.C.C.A.). The Justices were evenly divided on the question of whether the Nisga'a still held title and therefore the decision of the lower courts was upheld.

40 The Nisga'a final agreement is available on the Internet at http://www.ntc.bc.ca

government. The agreement recognizes that the Nisga'a nation has a right to self-government and the authority to make laws governing such matters as culture, language, and employment. The Nisga'a will continue to provide health, child welfare, and education services to their citizens.

In what is proving to be a contentious provision, only Nisga'a citizens[41] will be eligible to vote and run for office with regard to the Nisga'a central government and the four village governments. Non-Nisga'a persons will not be eligible to participate in elections for these core Nisga'a government structures.[42] The agreement stipulates that federal and provincial laws, including the Charter of Rights and Freedoms, will continue to apply to Nisga'a citizens and Nisga'a lands. The rights of non-Nisga'a owning and inhabiting lands within the territory have been preserved and such lands are excluded from the jurisdiction of the Nisga'a government . All inhabitants are entitled to make use of services and facilities provided by the Nisga'a such as municipal, health, and educational services. The Nisga'a will have direct taxation authority only with regard to Nisga'a citizens.

3. Reaction to the Nisga'a agreement

Initial responses to the agreement reached between the Nisga'a and the two levels of government were generally positive.[43] The settlement was seen as a signal achievement on the road to aboriginal self-government, heralding a decisive break with previous patterns of dependency, poverty, and despair. The Nisga'a would no longer be subject to the legal constraints of the federal Indian Act, under which Indian bands had for more than a century seen a large part of their lives controlled by government regulations administered by the Department of Indian Affairs and its omnipresent bureaucracy. They would also receive a significant land base, but one amounting to only one-eighth of their traditional territory. In return for this, resource rights and a financial package, the Nisga'a agreed to forgo their historical exemption

---

41 A Nisga'a citizen is defined as 'a citizen of the Nisga'a Nation as determined by Nisga'a law'. 'Nisga'a Nation' is defined as 'the collectivity of those Aboriginal people who share the language, culture, and laws of the Nisga'a Indians of the Nass Areas, and their descendants'. See *Nisga'a Final Agreement*, ch. 1, 'Definitions', p. 10.

42 The Agreement does, however, include provisions intended to ensure that the interests of non-native residents are taken into consideration. For example, it stipulates that Nisga'a governments will consult with individuals who are ordinarily resident within Nisga'a lands and who are not Nisga'a citizens about Nisga'a government decisions that directly and significantly affect them. Similarly, residents who are not Nisga'a will be able to participate in elected bodies that directly and significantly affect them. The means of participation can include opportunities to make representations, to vote for or seek election on Nisga'a public institutions, and to have the same means of appeal as Nisga'a citizens. See id., ch. 11, 'Nisga'a Government', p. 163.

43 See, for example, 'A treaty that breaks the chains of dependency' *Globe and Mail (Toronto)*, 25 July 1998, D2.

from all forms of taxation.[44] In short, all sides had compromised to achieve a reasonable solution to a longstanding dispute.

However, difficulties soon began to emerge. Opposition politicians in British Columbia questioned the deal, particularly those provisions which treated native and non-native residents differently. A strong ratification vote[45] by the Nisga'a did nothing to quell the debate, and positions became increasingly polarized.[46] Legal experts were marshalled on either side of the question of whether or not the agreement, once implemented would amount to an amendment to the Constitution of Canada and as such would require a province-wide referendum.[47] Finally, after threatening legal action if the provincial government failed to hold a referendum, the Liberal opposition leader filed a statement of claim with the British Columbia Supreme Court seeking a declaration that the Nisga'a final agreement was inconsistent with the provisions of the Constitution of Canada including the Charter of Rights and Freedoms.[48]

The reaction of the Nisga'a to the legal challenge was predictably angry.[49] From the beginning they had seen the agreement as a litmus test of the readiness of non-native society to acknowledge their status as a self-governing entity within the Canadian body politic. Native suspicions that racism

44 Aboriginals recognized as 'Indians' under the Indian Act and living on 'lands reserved for Indians' under the same Act are exempt from provincial and federal taxes. The exemption does not extend to so-called 'non-status' Indians or Metis, nor does it, in general, cover status Indians who are living off-reserve. Tax liability of aboriginals has become a contentious issue in recent years, as a result of significant out-migration from reserves to urban centres and the growth in native owned and operated businesses which (as long as they are headquartered on a reserve) can claim tax exempt status even if their activities extend off-reserve.

45 See 'Nisga'a ratify treaty with 70% in favour' *Globe and Mail (Toronto)*, 13 November 1998, A20.

46 See 'B.C. rhetoric turns inflammatory in debate over Nisga'a treaty' *Globe and Mail (Toronto)*, 14 November 1998, A10.

47 See 'Pressure rises for referendum on Nisga'a' *Globe and Mail (Toronto)*, 12 November 1998, A21. 'A province-wide referendum on the proposed Nisga'a treaty would lead to a poisonous, racially divisive debate, Premier Glen Clark says. Mr. Clark is under mounting pressure to give British Columbians a vote on the treaty covering 6,000 Nisga'a in the remote northwest of the province . . . However, Mr. Clark said his government has not intention of putting the matter to a vote. "Frankly, I think that would lead to a racial debate from which I think it would be very difficult to recover", he told a supportive public meeting in his . . . riding.'

48 The claim states that the deal is unconstitutional because 'it would establish a Nisga'a government with authority to make laws, which in specified areas of jurisdiction would prevail over federal and provincial laws, and because it would breach the guarantee of democratic rights under the Charter by denying non-Nisga'a citizens the right to vote or participate as elected members in the Nisga'a government. The statement of claim suggests that valid ratification of the Nisga'a Final Agreement would require an amendment to the Constitution of Canada, and a province-wide referendum. See 'B.C. court to consider constitutional basis for Nisga'a treaty' *Globe and Mail (Toronto)*, 20 October 1998, A8.

49 See 'Nisga'a treaty challenge "dangerous"' *Toronto Star*, 20 October 1998, A6.

continued to play a part in frustrating their desires was also perhaps understandable in the context of the province's historical treatment of minority groups. Meanwhile, the present British Columbia government, which has been more sympathetic to minority concerns than some of its predecessors but whose level of public support is extremely low, indicated that the legal challenge would not deflect it from its plans to proceed with ratification.[50] It is also clear that the federal government will introduce implementing legislation in the months ahead.

It is unfortunate that final efforts to resolve the longstanding grievances of the Nisga'a have to some extent been hijacked by political agendas. However, it needs to be acknowledged that the ingredients of the settlement embody significant policy choices. For example, the award to the Nisga'a of fishing and timber rights will necessarily restrict the current or future rights of non-natives resident in the area. Moreover, to the extent that the agreement departs from generally accepted principles of equal treatment for all Canadians (notably with regard to the proposed restrictions on the right to vote) it can be viewed as an instance of group rights trumping individual rights, and as such hardly likely to pass without comment.

CONCLUDING OBSERVATIONS

In the present article I have endeavoured to illustrate some features of the current human rights landscape in Canada through an examination of three cases. One involves an issue of freedom of speech arising from a classic confrontation between political opponents of a foreign regime and law enforcement agencies at home. Claims to equality of treatment feature in the two other cases considered. They are at the centre of the PSAC complaint and have become a factor in the latter stages of the Nisga'a settlement. The Charter of Rights and Freedoms continues to serve as the vehicle guaranteeing human rights (or more accurately, civil and political rights) and has been invoked in both the APEC and Nisga'a disputes, in the former to support a claim to redress by victims of alleged police abuse of power and in the latter, perhaps ironically, as an adjunct to efforts to delay and possibly undermine an agreement aimed at cementing intergroup relations.

Although the sample of cases considered has been small, some observations may be ventured. First, the human rights model in Canada seems to work best when dealing with claims that fall most clearly under the head of civil and political rights and for which there is a fairly high level of public understanding. Directing pepper spray towards an ostensibly non-violent group of protestors is something the public can readily comprehend. The issues presented by the APEC complaints are thus amenable to an adjudication

50 id., A8

69

whose results are likely to be accepted.[51] By contrast, the principle of equality which lays at the base of the PSAC pay equity complaint has failed to carry the day notwithstanding the complainants' success in arguing the legal merits of their case. As has been suggested earlier, there are several reasons for this. The issue of cost is, of course, a factor in the government's strategy of attrition. But its ability to delay resolution of the matter in spite of losing every procedural and substantive battle along the way is undoubtedly aided by the lack of resonance the issues at stake have with the majority of the public.

The PSAC complaint points up a further limitation on the effectiveness of human rights machinery arising from weaknesses in the adjudication process. The tribunal in the PSAC case may have been thorough in its approach, permitting more than 250 days of hearing over a period of more than six years before arriving at its decision, but a portion of the delay was attributable to a leisurely schedule adopted by its members. Although a human rights tribunal has some of the powers of a court of law, its members are not judges but appointees of the government of the day and its independence has been challenged in the past. Over the years, tribunal decisions have been of variable quality, and it was therefore not altogether implausible for the government to attempt to justify its decision to seek judicial review in the PSAC case by pointing to the need for clarity in an area of the law where the impact of rulings could be dramatic but available jurisprudence was extremely limited.[52]

A final issue I wish briefly to address concerns the approach to aboriginal self-government embodied in the Nisga'a final agreement and the principle of equality. The denial of the right to vote to Canadian citizens living in the region who happen to be non-natives does, of course, suggest an incompatibility with Charter guarantees of equality, at the formal level. But equality law in Canada has long favoured a purposive approach in which the search is for substance rather than the form of equality. Without wishing to prejudge the outcome of the current court challenge to the Nisga'a agreement, some general points can be made. First, aboriginal people in Canada have been treated unequally, in both a legal and social sense, since the first Indian Act was passed in 1876. For example, until 1960, the majority of aboriginal people were not eligible to vote in federal elections, nor could they manage their own reserve lands or money. In fact the Indian Act which

---

51 I am referring here to the question of whether the police acted in a way to deny the complainants' rights to freedom of expression, assembly and association as guaranteed by s. 2 of the Charter (see n. 12 above). On the issue of whether political considerations (rather than security concerns) governed police actions, adjudication may be more difficult. An issue of institutional bias may also arise, given that the police respondents in the APEC complaint and the RCMP Public Complaints Commission tasked with adjudicating are both ultimately accountable to the same Minister.

52 Recent amendments to the Canadian Human Rights Act have provided for the establishment of a human rights tribunal with additional numbers of full-time members. See Bill S-5, Introduced in First Session, 36th Parliament, 46 Eliz.II, 1997.

continues to govern the lives of most aboriginal Canadians is a statute that embodies the idea of separateness in treatment of native people.

There is therefore something of a paradox in invoking a perceived denial of equality to a small number of non-natives resident in territory traditionally occupied by the Nisga'a as a reason to block the latter's right to self government. It is appropriate here to return to the notion of human dignity that has underpinned human rights instruments since the Universal Declaration of Human Rights in 1948. It is this which has led to reaffirmation of the need to give economic, social, and cultural rights a level of protection equal to that afforded political and civil rights. For the Nisga'a, the social and cultural autonomy embodied in the claims agreement is an important, perhaps essential ingredient for their survival as a people. It is hoped that these considerations will be given appropriate weight when current challenges to the agreement are heard by the courts. In the words of Thomas Berger, who as lawyer and judge has long been associated with the native cause:

> You can't subjugate a people who happen to be of one race, take their land, destroy their institutions and then turn around a hundred years later and say 'To allow you to restore the institutions you once had would be contrary to our principles. We don't hold with race-based institutions. It's bad luck that you were all of one race when we came here so, we are going to deny you the right to govern yourselves on your own land, except to the extend that we decide from time to time to delegate power to you – power that we can withdraw at any time'.[53]

---

53 See 'Nisga'a won't knuckle under' *Vancouver Sun*, 29 October 1998, A19.

JOURNAL OF LAW AND SOCIETY
VOLUME 26, NUMBER 1, MARCH 1999
ISSN: 0263–323X, pp. 72–85

The Human Rights Act – A New Equity or a New Opiate: Reinventing Justice or Repackaging State Control?

LUKE CLEMENTS*

The proposed incorporation of the European Convention on Human Rights into the main stream of the United Kingdom's common law system has a number of historical parallels. This article considers what can usefully be drawn from these parallels and then analyses why the modern state feels impelled to take (what appears to be) such a fundamental constitutional step. It considers whether the incorporation agenda is in fact a more subtle discourse initiated by the 'Establishment' and designed to divert attention from matters of greater sensitivity to the state.

INTRODUCTION

The White Paper, *Rights Brought Home*, asserts that the Human Rights Act 1998, will make it possible for people to invoke their basic human rights in any proceedings against the state, and in adjudicating upon such proceedings, the courts will be *bound to give precedence* (my emphasis) to upholding these rights.[1] The Act will (the White Paper continues) go 'far beyond' the present situation whereby the courts can only consider arguments concerning the European Convention on Human Rights when resolving any ambiguity in a legislative provision.[2] Few lawyers could seriously question that a change to United Kingdom law of such proportions would indeed be a truly radical development.

An old fashioned, by-standing anarchist might in consequence be moved to question whether this much trumpeted Act will in practice measure up to the 'hype'; whether it will in reality prove to be a radical new equity; and if so, why does the state feel it necessary to take such action; and, assuming

---

1 Home Office, *Rights Brought Home: The Human Rights Bill* (1997; Cm. 3782) 2, and adopting the conceit of substituting the phrase 'basic human rights' for 'the Convention'.
2 id., para. 2.7.

* Solicitor and Senior Research Fellow, Cardiff Law School, P.O Box 427, Museum Avenue, Cardiff CF1 1XD, Wales

that the pressure for reform was irresistible, why has the state responded with the Human Rights Act 1998? Given the classic view that the state protects itself, the Act appears to provide the anarchist with the tools, not only to challenge the state but also to set about dismantling it. This paper seeks to address these questions.

HISTORICAL PARALLELS

Whilst allusions to the Convention's ancestry have not always been positive,[3] its historic importance has seldom been questioned. In 1987, Sir Edward Gardner QC, when introducing one of the many[4] Bills which sought to incorporate the Convention into United Kingdom law, described 'the language of the Convention' as 'language which echoes right down the corridors of history'. Its language, he continued, 'goes deep into our history and as far back as the Magna Carta'.[5] Sir William Holdsworth also noted the resonance of the Great Charter with recent human rights instruments and suggested that its closest contemporary parallel was 'the legislation resulting from those modern international Conventions which have formulated rules of international law'.[6]

It is clear, of course, what was 'in it' for the state when King John reached his compromise with the barons at Runnymede. In similar vein we can look back and see relatively clearly the political imperatives for the radical state action that resulted in the Bill of Rights and indeed in the development of equity; it is not however quite so clear what is 'in it' for the state this time around. The reforms heralded by the White Paper reach further than the traditional response of changing the power relations between the key stakeholders in the state[7] in that they appear to give non-stakeholders the power to attack the state itself.

Although the Convention undoubtedly owes much to the Bill of Rights[8] (for instance, its prohibition on cruel and unusual punishments,[9] freedom

3 Lord Bingham, Lord Chief Justice, in his Denning lecture, 'The European Convention on Human Rights: Time to Incorporate' (2 March 1993) referred to Lord Chancellor Jowitt's description of the Commission on Human Rights as a 'sort of Court of Star Chamber' (published in *Human Rights in the United Kingdom*, eds. R. Gordon and R. Wilmot-Smith (1996).
4 Lord Wade, Lord Boxbourne, Lord Scarman, and Lord Lester (on two occasions) introduced similar Bills which were generally 'mutilated by wrecking amendments'; for an account of such action, see A. Lester, 'The Mouse that Roared: The Human Rights Bill 1995' [1995] *Public Law* 198.
5 E. Gardner, 109 *H.C. Debs.*, col. 1224 (6 February 1987).
6 W. Holdsworth, *The History of English Law* vol. 2 (4th edn., 1936) 210.
7 Although an increase in judicial power at the expense of the executive would indeed do this.
8 See, for instance, C.R. Lovell, *English Constitutional and Legal History* (1962) 393 and following.
9 Clause 10, compare article 3 of the Convention.

73

of speech,[10] and the right to free elections[11]) the genesis of the 1998 Act can most usefully be contrasted with rise of equity. As with the 1998 Act, the pressures which led to the growth of equity were not accompanied by the threat of civil insurrection, unlike those which presaged the reforms of 1215 and 1688. Equity eventually came to trump the inflexible and unfair doctrines of the common law in much the same way that the Convention can be seen as injecting new human-rights-based principles into a legal system fixated with the concept of ownership and property.

Austin observed[12] that equity 'arose from the sulkiness and obstinacy of the Common Law Courts which refused to suit themselves to the changes which took place in the opinion and circumstances of society'. Few non-lawyers would disagree with the proposition that domestic law has signally failed to 'suit itself' to the radical changes that have occurred in the latter part of this century. A law that has balked at the publication of *Spycatcher* when it was freely available on the internet, which allowed fairy-tale libel awards,[13] denied children[14] and their putative fathers[15] access to court, acquits violent step-parents,[16] and gives immunity to negligent police forces.[17] A law that is not only sulky, but one dominated by a judiciary, who like the Judges of Common Pleas, obstinately cling to the view that it is an unparalleled good. Judges in wigs and silk stockings; judges who have presided over a catalogue of infamous miscarriages of justice; judges who, when presented with the 'appalling vista'[18] of an establishment cover up, draw the drapes; a judiciary that has merely 'paid lip service to fundamental freedoms'.[19]

Just as the Judicature Acts of 1873 and 1875 ended the uncomfortable and bitter co-existence of equity and the common law, so too will the 1998 Act conclude an equally undignified period of rivalry between the Convention and our common law. Whilst the common law's negative co-habitation with equity lasted for considerably longer than that with the Convention, the present cohabitation has been no less acrimonious. Until comparatively recently, it took considerable courage for an advocate to refer to the Convention, in a United Kingdom court. With a few honourable exceptions, the judicial response was a condescending or contemptuous rebuke. That the Convention struck an unpleasant chord with most judges, is unsurprising in that it was something about which they knew little or nothing and was 'foreign'. Notwithstanding this hostility, references to the

10 Clause 9 (albeit parliamentary speech), compare article 10.
11 Clause 8, compare article 3 of protocol 1.
12 J. Austin, *Lectures on Jurisprudence* (3rd edn., 1869) 635.
13 *Tolstoy* v. *UK*, 20 E.H.R.R. 442.
14 *P., P. & T.* v. *UK*, 22 E.H.R.R. CD 148.
15 *O., H., W., B., R.* v. *UK* 10 E.H.R.R. 29–95.
16 *A.* v. *UK* European Court of Human Rights 23.9.98.
17 *Osman* v. *UK* European Court of Human Rights 28.10.98.
18 Per Lord Denning MR in *McIlkenny and others* v. *Chief Constable West Midlands Police Force* (1980).
19 J.A.G. Griffith, *The Politics of the Judiciary* (4th edn., 1991) 281.

74

Convention in domestic proceedings have grown exponentially[20] such that it would today be rare indeed to observe a sitting of the Divisional Court and not hear it mentioned.

The administration of the Crown Office[21] List, with its idiosyncratic procedures, its cadre of specialist public law judges, and its rapidly developing supervisory jurisdiction is markedly 'separate' from the other business of the High Court. It can, and does, scrutinize non-Divisional Court judgments. For instance, it can 'stay' and effectively cancel an eviction order issued by another High Court Judge[22] – not by applying the 'rules of equity' but by application of a similar legal fiction, the *Wednesbury*[23] principles. In this 'separateness' we hear echoes of Palgrave's lament (1834) that:

> it must appear a singular anomaly to a foreigner, when he is informed that our English tribunals are marshalled in opposite, and even, hostile ranks: guided by maxims so discrepant, that the title which enables a suitor to obtain a decree without the slightest doubt or hesitation if he files a bill in Equity, ensures a judgment against him should he appear as a plaintiff in a declaration at common law.[24]

The similarities between the Acts themselves (the Human Rights Act 1998 and the Judicature Act 1873[25]) are marked. Just as section 2 of the 1998 Act allows Convention law to be considered in domestic law courts and section 3 for it (in effect) to take precedence[26] where conflict arises, so too did the 1873 Act apply for equity. Section 24 provided for the rules of equity to be administered in all common law courts and sections 11 and 25 provided that 'in all matters, not hereinbefore particularly mentioned, in which there is any conflict or variance between the Rules of Equity and the rules of Common Law, with reference to the same matter, the Rules of Equity shall prevail'.

The development of Convention law jurisprudence within domestic courts parallels the development of equity; both have arisen organically in response to social forces pressing for the redistribution of 'legal fairness'. Equity only superficially touched upon constitutional issues, and its redistributive effect did not extend significantly beyond the propertied classes.[27] The growth of the Convention's influence in the United Kingdom is, however, primarily a facet of the emergence (and extraordinary growth[28]) of public law. In the

---

20 Murray Hunt charts the growth of references to the Convention in reported decisions in his *Using Human Rights Law in English Courts* (1997) from one in 1964 to nine in 1975 to fifty-eight in 1996.
21 Which administers the judicial review and other public law proceedings in the High Court.
22 See, for instance, *R. v. Lincolnshire County Council* (1995), reported in *Times* 22 September 1995.
23 *Associated Provincial Picture Houses Ltd. v. Wednesbury Corporation* [1948] 1 K.B. 223.
24 *The Council I*; quoted by Holdsworth, op. cit., n. 6, vol. 1, p. 635.
25 36, 37 Victoria c. 66.
26 Section 3(1) provides that 'so far as it is possible to do so, primary legislation and subordinate legislation must be read and given effect in a way which is compatible with the Convention rights.'
27 The 'realigned property classes' of Chrisopher Hill's *Liberty against the Law* (1996) 332.
28 See, for instance, L. Bridges, G. Mesazaros, and M. Sunkin, *Judicial Review in Perspective* (2nd ed., 1995).

75

last thirty years, judicial review has itself 'effected a wholesale revolution in our constitutional structure'.[29] In this guise, domestic Convention law jurisprudence, riding on the back of the phenomenal growth in public law proceedings, constitutes a radical new equity of fundamental importance. The Human Rights Act however (again in marked similarity to the Judicature Acts) does not presage this radical development – as it is a development that has, in large measure already occurred; the horse has already bolted.

REINING IN THE USE OF CONVENTION LAW

Whilst a legislative response to this largely unplanned organic jurisprudential phenomenon is inevitable, slamming the stable door is not of course an option. In the circumstances, our jaundiced anarchist might warn us to beware of 'the Establishment' bearing sugar lumps and a saddle.

From such a cynical perspective the sweetener is of course the acceptance by the 1998 Act of the right to refer to the Convention in all domestic cases; in reality however this is only accelerating the inevitable. From the government's perspective, the right to invoke the Convention in domestic proceedings is not a step into the unknown, since (as noted above) it has now had thirty years of experience of such challenges. There are also collateral benefits to such a relaxation of the rules, not least the avoidance of the constant stream of embarrassing Strasbourg judgements

'Avoidance of embarrassing Strasbourg judgements' does not inevitably translate into the domestic courts reaching the same decision as would have Strasbourg. In practice we are likely to see judges making it significantly more difficult for cases to succeed in Strasbourg: beefing up the contra-Convention arguments (rather than merely refusing to listen to them). Few people could reasonably believe that had the Convention been incorporated into to domestic law that the present House of Lords would have found article 2 violated by the Gibraltar killings (*McCann and others* v. *UK* (1995)[30]) or article 6 violated by the refusal of access to a lawyer under the Criminal Evidence (Northern Ireland) Act 1988 (*Murray* v. *UK* (1996)[31]) or a violation of the principle of non-self incrimination in *Saunders* v. *UK* (1996)[32] or the right to legal aid in poll tax evasion cases (*Benham* v. *UK* (1996)[33]), and so on; the recent catalogue of humiliations is extensive.

Camelot Group v. *Centaur Ltd* (1998)[34] is a foretaste of what we are more likely to witness. Here the plaintiff lottery company sought and obtained an

29 A.H. Hammond, 'Judicial Review: the continuing interplay between law and policy' [1998] *Public Law* 34.
30 21 E.H.R.R. 97.
31 22 E.H.R.R. 29.
32 23 E.H.R.R. 313.
33 22 E.H.R.R. 293.
34 [1998] 1 All E.R. 251.

injunction requiring the defendant publishing company to identify the person who leaked confidential information to it (which the defendant then published). Notwithstanding the fact that such an injunction flew in the face of a recent Strasbourg decision,[35] the Court of Appeal found in favour of the plaintiff, relying heavily upon a domestic decision[36] which had been specifically criticized by the European Court of Human Rights. Viewed charitably, the Court of Appeal's judgment is a workmanlike attempt at 'Strasbourg proofing': paying lip-service to fundamental freedoms but coming to the same old reactionary common law conclusion. Viewed less charitably, it is a defiant gesture to the Human Rights Court.

Even where the domestic courts are prepared to show less contempt for their European comrades their comments do not, in general, inspire confidence as to how they will discharge their post-incorporation powers. In *R. v. Ministry of Defence ex p. Smith (and others)*,[37] for example, the point in issue concerned the Ministry's blanket ban upon homosexuals serving in the armed forces. At first instance[38] there was a difference of opinion between Simon Brown LJ and Curtis J. Simon Brown LJ intimated that, if the Convention had been incorporated into United Kingdom law, he would have found the policy to be incompatible with it; whereas Curtis J considered the policy consistent with the Convention and the Court of Appeal rather limply questioned the 'utility of such a debate'.[39]

Having discovered the sugar lump not to be as sweet as one first expected, there is then the saddle. There are many ways that the state can harness this hitherto largely uncontrolled development. Perhaps most effective of all is the maintenance of public ignorance. Whilst every United States schoolchild is inculcated with the importance of their Constitutional rights, and whilst we learn that the Lord Chancellor's Department have set aside £4.5 million to be spent on judicial training, nothing appears to have been instigated to ensure a wider public appreciation.

On the related and highly relevant issue of a Freedom of Information Act, Justice Michael Kirby has warned that the passage of such measures does not in itself work the necessary revolution in culture and attitudes of public administration. Pointing to the lack of publicity and education programmes that accompanied the Australian legislation, he warned that if little is done to promote knowledge of the reform and to enhance the citizen's view of the new rights, then they are unlikely to be put to general use.[40]

Restricting litigant access to the new procedures can be achieved by savagely cutting back on the availability of legal aid, and this is precisely

35 *Goodwin* v. *UK* (1996); 22 E.H.R.R. 123
36 *X Ltd.* v. *Morgan-Grampian (Publishers Ltd.)* [1990] 2 All E.R 1, [1991] 1 A.C. 1.
37 [1996] 1 All E.R. 257.
38 [1995] 4 All E.R. 427.
39 Per Henry LJ at p 272a
40 M. Kirby, 'Freedom of Information – The Seven Deadly Sins' [1998] issue 3 *European Human Rights Law Rev.* 245.

what the government is doing. Indeed there are many lawyers who believe that the reason why the Act's implementation in England and Wales has been delayed until (at least) year 2000, is to ensure that it only comes into effect once these much criticized cutbacks have occurred. The reforms will reduce the number of law firms offering legal aid from about 11,000 to about 3,000 and have been the subject of significant judicial criticism. We see here the idea of bringing rights home, but making sure that poor people can't use them: a strong resonance again with equity.

The legal aid changes have attracted the criticism of the Lord Chief Justice, who expressed his anxiety about them undermining the ability of 'the least affluent in society . . . to defend their rights and make claims'[41] and of his considerable misgivings about the proposed withdrawal of all legal aid from money and damages cases, suggesting that this reform could also have the effect of excluding certain sections of the public from justice. The government's view is that in such cases the applicant should rely upon a conditional fee agreement (CFA) with the lawyer. Since CFAs are only viable when the lawyer believes that the litigation has good prospects of success and that the compensation will be sufficient to pay a 'success fee', there is really little or no prospect of CFAs being of anything other than theoretically available for Convention proceedings.[42] The outcome of such proceedings is particularly difficult to predict (as evidenced by the large number of occasions that the former Court and Commission of Human Rights disagreed), and in general (as discussed below), even where an applicant's rights have been found to be violated, no compensation is awarded. Such awards as are made are generally parsimonious by domestic standards.

A consequence of the removal of all money and damages cases from legal aid assistance is that in general, in order for a poor person to obtain legal assistance (to pursue a Convention claim in the domestic courts) he or she would have to abandon any claim for damages. This is not only an extraordinary state of affairs, it is in itself a substantial and utterly unreasonable form of discrimination. Unfortunately the legal aid rules have a further unpleasant surprise for such a would-be litigant. Even if the money claim is abandoned, the applicant still has to establish to the satisfaction of the Legal Aid Board that there are reasonable prospects of success and that a fee-paying person of average means would be likely to pursue such a claim. Very few people of average means would ever contemplate suing the government in situations where there was no possibility of obtaining some financial relief; and, in any event, even fewer lawyers could honestly establish to their own satisfaction (let alone the Legal Aid Board's) that a Convention claim had 60 per cent or better prospects of succeeding (at one stage the government

41 Lord Bingham at the Lord Chief Justice's Annual Press Conference 95/39, in *Law Society's Gazette*, 14 October 1998, 5.
42 As indeed they are already 'theoretically available' for applications to the European Court of Human Rights by virtue of the Conditional Fees Agreements Regulations 1995, appendix 3; although there is no evidence that they have ever been of any use in such proceedings.

78

was suggesting that this should be a better than 75 per cent chance of success). If the High Court and Court of Appeal had significant doubts about the situation in *ex p. Smith* (as clear a case as one might have thought possible) then what possibility is there of being confident in lesser cases?

Not only were equity's improvements largely reserved for the upper middle classes, the procedures for invoking and pursing them were the substance of fable; the 'tens of thousands of Chancery folio-pages' of Jarndyce and Jarndyce. The rules of this particular game are reasonably well defined: in response to pressure from an influential minority, legislate new 'rights' and then make it virtually impossible to enforce them. The absence of legal aid is only a major impediment if the law and court procedures are sufficiently restrictive, complex, and long-winded to defeat all but the most determined of litigants in person.

The first of this further basket of obstructionist measures consists of restricting *locus standi*. Conscious of this danger, Sir Stephen Sedley, when expressing his concern that society's losers and winners will merely become the same losers and winners under a Human Rights Act, suggested that this be tackled by the development of a 'more sophisticated concept of *locus standi*'.[43] Far from adopting such an approach, the Human Rights Act 1998 imposes significantly more restrictive *locus* criteria than the Divisional Court. Section 7 is admirably obstructionist, in that applicants can only rely on the Convention in domestic proceedings if they are 'victims' within the meaning ascribed to this concept by the European Court of Human Rights.[44]

De Smith, Woolf, and Jowell[45] highlight 'the substantial arguments in favour of adopting a generous approach to standing' as there is a need in public law proceedings 'to encourage and not to discourage public-spirited individuals and groups, even though they are not directly affected by the action which is being taken, to challenge unlawful administrative action'. If there are strict rules of standing, then (they observe) 'there will be the risk that no one will be in a position to bring proceedings to test the lawfulness of obvious illegality or questionable legality'. It is this view which has so far predominated within Crown Office proceedings such that Greenpeace had standing to challenge the legality of testing THORP and the World Development Movement Ltd. had standing to challenge United Kingdom grant-aid for a Malaysian dam. Such liberalization of *locus standi* does not appear to have caused undue problems for the domestic courts (there being, as de Smith points out, 'other safeguards to protect the courts from unmeritorious challenges'[46]).

43 S. Sedley, 'First Steps Towards a Constitutional Bill of Rights' [1997] issue 5 *European Human Rights Law Rev.* 458.
44 S. 7(6) Human Rights Act 1998.
45 S.A. de Smith, Lord Woolf and J. Jowell, *Judicial Review of Administrative Action* (5th edn., 1995) at 101.
46 id.

In contrast, Strasbourg's criteria for 'sufficient standing' requires that applicants establish that they have been directly affected by the matter complained of; that they can show themselves to be actual victims.[47] In consequence, it has been held that a law not significantly different to the no-pass laws formerly in South Africa cannot be challenged unless someone who has actually been victimized by it is prepared to do so.[48] The fact that such an abhorrent law exists is not sufficient in itself to permit one of a class of the persons potentially affected to complain.

Of course such severe *locus* restrictions can be mitigated by the establishment of a powerful public interest 'Commission' capable of instituting representative proceedings where no victim is prepared (or able) to litigate or indeed in the absence of any identifiable victim. The Disability Discrimination Act 1995 (a classic example of 'reluctant' legislation) was grudgingly enacted in response to pressure from an influential minority, and, accordingly, its new 'rights' were made very difficult to enforce. Although the lack of a supervising Disability Rights Commission was fiercely criticized by the Labour opposition as evidence of the Conservative government's lack of commitment to the legislation,[49] the Labour government has ruled out a Human Rights Commission for the 1998 Act.

Lord Lester, who has perhaps done more than any other lawyer to promote the cause of incorporation, has argued that without a Human Rights Commission 'there could be no coherent legal strategy, and individuals might be worse off than at present'.[50] The importance of such a Commission has been stressed by a number of other commentators, particularly the Institute for Public Policy Research[51] and the present Master of the Rolls, Lord Woolf, in whose view the case for a Commission is 'utterly convincing'.[52]

As noted above, the artificial suppression of the level of damages can be a particularly effective impediment to enforcing rights. The Disability Discrimination Act 1995 achieved this by specifying the maximum level of damages available for certain violations;[53] this has the benefit of putting nearly all such claims below the 'small claims limit' and thereby (again) excluding, not only the possibility of legal aid, but also the likelihood of being awarded costs – even if the claim were successful. Of course, if the level of damages is sufficiently low it can, in itself, act as a fundamental disincentive to enforcing rights.

---

47 See, for instance, *Leigh, Guardian Newspapers Ltd. & the Observer Ltd.* v. *UK* 38 DR 74.
48 *Ruby Smith* v. *UK* Application 18401/91; decision 6.5.93.
49 DfEE press release 21 July 1998 'New Commission To Promote Disabled People's Rights'.
50 Lester, op. cit., n. 4.
51 Institute for Public Policy Research, *A British Bill of Rights* (2nd ed., 1996), and see, also, S. Spencer and I. Bynoe, 'A Human Rights Commission for the United Kingdom – Some Options' [1997] issue 2 *European Human Rights Law Rev.* 152.
52 As quoted in 95/39, *Law Society's Gazette*, 14 October 1998, 14.
53 Sched. 3, para. 7.

True to form, s. 8(4) Human Rights Act 1998 stipulates that in assessing the level of damages to be awarded for a violation of a Convention right, the domestic courts shall be guided by Strasbourg awards and not our own. There is a 'low rate of success in obtaining compensation awards'[54] in Strasbourg; in general when the Court finds the Convention to have been violated, it rules that this finding is in itself sufficient compensation for the applicant. Even where an award is made, it is low or very low by domestic standards. A recent review of Strasbourg compensation judgments[55] voiced 'serious concerns about the consistency' of the decisions; noted that the Court was very reluctant to make awards to convicted prisoners, and that it never awarded more than approximately 50 per cent of the amounts claimed by applicants.

The importance of simplifying domestic procedures to facilitate effective individual access to Convention rights has been stressed by Sir Stephen Sedley.[56] Anticipating incorporation he pointed to the need for a system of 'leap-frog appeals to the House of Lords with a system of referrals now familiar in the context of the ECJ'. Complex procedures are of course particularly effective in obstructing access to justice, and especially potent when combined with delay.

The Human Rights Act 1998 has the very antithesis of a fast-track or leap-frog procedure. Take, for instance, an applicant, who is defending a summary prosecution on the grounds that the primary legislation is incompatible with the Convention.[57] She or he must first argue the issue before the magistrates. Since this is doomed to failure (as the Act precludes justices from making declarations of incompatibility), it is likely that legal aid will refused on the 'merits' ground. After conviction and sentence the defendant will presumably have to invoke the daunting 'case stated' procedure[58] in an effort to get the matter before the High Court where the 'incompatibility' issue can be considered. It is difficult to envisage a more sterile, long-winded, and deliberately obstructionist procedure, particularly as the majority of potential defendants will be ineligible (on financial grounds) for any form of legal aid.

Not only has the opportunity to create a simplified and streamlined court procedure been rejected, but it also appears likely that domestic courts will insist (by practice direction or otherwise) on Convention cases adopting yet more complex procedures. In *ex p. Smith (and others)*[59] for instance, Henry

---

54 A.R. Mowbray, 'The European Court of Human Rights' Approach to Just Satisfaction' [1997] *Public Law* 647.

55 id.

56 S. Sedley, 'A Bill of Rights for Britain' [1997] issue 5 *European Human Rights Law Rev.* 458.

57 S. 4 Human Rights Act 1998.

58 A procedure of some antiquity, originally introduced by the Court of Chancery in the seventeenth century.

59 [1996] 1 All E.R. 257.

81

LJ suggested that upon incorporation the court might require considerably more material than the adversarial system normally provides, such as *'Brandis* briefs'.

The final and most daunting obstacle of all is the ability of the state to simply ignore Convention decisions. The general perception is that the United Kingdom plays by the rules in Strasbourg and will do likewise when the Convention is incorporated. This belief has been so oft repeated that it has entered into the legal folklore; a recent example being the assertion that the 'British Government has, without a single exception, implemented the findings of the Strasbourg Court, even when hostile, so the same should apply under the New Act'.[60] This unfortunately is not the case. When the issue gets close to the true sensitivity of the state, that is, terrorism and secrecy, then we see decidedly unsportsmanlike responses. It is certainly the case that the government has refused (and continues to refuse) to comply with the European Court of Human Rights decision in *Brogan* v. *UK* (1988)[61] concerning the prevention of terrorism legislation. What is perhaps more revealing of the state's vulnerability is the United Kingdom's failure to comply with access to information decisions. *Gaskin* v. *UK* (1989) concerned the relatively innocuous matter of access to social services files, and yet the government has still not brought domestic legislation onto line with the judgment.[62] Considerably more of the state's soft underbelly was exposed in *Malone* v. *UK* (1984)[63] concerning the tapping of telephone conversations; the United Kingdom's response, the Interception of Communications Act 1985, was minimalistic if not clearly deficient[64] and now further exacerbated by the Security Services Act 1996.[65] An equally inadequate response to a disclosure of information decision by Strasbourg[66] came in *Harman* v. *UK* (1984).[67]

---

60 F. Bennion, 'Which sort of Human Rights Act?' (1998) 148 *New Law J.* 488.
61 11 E.H.R.R. 117.
62 The offending statute, the Access to Files Act 1987 is in the process of being repealed by the Data Protection Act 1998 but the new Act appears to suffer from precisely the same shortcomings as the 1987 legislation.
63 13 E.H.R.R. 448.
64 See L. Lustgarten and I. Leigh, *In from the cold: National Security and Parliamentary Democracy* (1994) and *Halford* v. *UK* 24 E.H.R.R. 523.
65 An Act which provides for 'the carry over of powers, which are unhappily necessary in the context of national security, into a policing function enabling a member of the Executive to sanction entry into private property without prior judicial warrant' per Lord Browne-Wilkinson, 573 *H.L. Official Reports*, col. 1044, and see P. Duffy and M. Hunt, 'Goodbye *Entick* v. *Carrington*: the Security Service Act 1996 [1997] issue 1 *European Human Rights Law Rev.* 11.
66 In this case, the *European Commission of Human Rights*.
67 38 DR 53 and see the Commissions criticism of s. 10 Contempt of Court Act 1981 in *Goodwin* v. *UK* 22 E.H.R.R. 123, at 135.

82

The rapid development of public law and Convention jurisprudence within domestic law has resulted in the emergence of a radical new equity. Sooner or later this needed to be formalized and 'controlled'. It would be wrong however to suggest that matters had reached a critical point at which a legislative response was unavoidable. The system could have moved on for a few more years, secure in the knowledge that the present House of Lords would do its best to keep hold of the reins.

Cabinet secrecy means that it will be many years before we can discover what were precisely the political considerations which finally tilted the balance in favour of incorporation. Lord Lester, in his analysis of the events that led to the signing of the optional protocol on individual petitions in 1966, has shown that these political considerations are not always entirely predictable.[68] Most of these considerations, however, point towards incorporation as having distinct political benefits for the present government. Having endured almost twenty years in opposition, its manifesto commitment to constitutional change is hardly surprising. Incorporating the Convention is more likely to disembowel the Adam Smith ship of state than New Labour's flotilla. As an image, 'Europeanism' is seen as modern and different, and one should never underestimate the enormous importance of image management today – given the extraordinary lengths to which politicians and increasingly judges and the Establishment go to do it.

Incorporation will also underpin the wider constitutional reform agenda which has at times been seen as lacking philosophical gravitas. It will provide a piece of intellectual substance for the civil servants who are concerned about repositioning the state merely on 'fashion' grounds. The Convention has proved a vitalizing force without being too disturbing. It is in keeping with the prevailing liberalism and Europeanism of the intellectual élite and very much at odds with the unlovely right-wing populists so abhorred by the educated Establishment.

THE OPIATE

The legal impediments to enforcing Convention rights are daunting today and will be hardly less daunting when the Human Rights Act 1998 comes into force. The anarchist would be reassured to have his or her prejudices reinforced, witnessing the state diverting and confusing: confusing by the imposition of a number of significant obstacles to accessing this radical new equity; diverting by using the Human Rights Act as an opiate. The problem with challenging state action does not stem from a dearth of legal tools (as

---

68 'U.K. Acceptance of the Strasbourg Jurisdiction: What Really went on in Whitehall in 1965' [1998] *Public Law* 237.

83

we have seen, judicial review and the development of Convention law has been growing apace); the problem is 'evidence': of having sufficient information to prove one's case.

Whilst history might well show the anarchist's response to be wrong, here at the beginning of 1999, it does appear relatively convincing. The opiate diverts attention from the pressing realities; the state's obsession with secrecy. We have just witnessed a French *Chambre d'Accusation* take the extraordinary step of refusing to agree to the extradition of David Shayler to England. A former MI5 agent, he had been charged under the Official Secrets Acts with disclosing confidential information. Judge Ponroy accepted, however, that the purpose behind his disclosures was to expose incompetence and bungling within the security services, and thus the charges were political in nature. Her judgment joins that of the Australian Courts in Peter Wright's (1987) *Spycatcher* débâcle[69] and the infamous prosecutions of Clive Ponting (1985) and Sarah Tisdall (1984) who had the temerity to expose, not merely incompetence, but deception. An *Independent* newspaper leader,[70] following David Shayler's acquittal, observed how curious it was that both the present Prime Minister and Home Secretary (who had sought Shayler's extradition) had, whilst in opposition, opposed the use of the Official Secrets Act without a public interest defence, but had both changed their minds in office.

On the same day, Parliament was debating the failure of the government to include a Freedom of Information Act in the Queen's Speech.[71] David Clarke MP had, as Chancellor of the Duchy of Lancaster, overseen the preparation of such a Bill, despite civil service obstruction and substantial opposition from the Home Secretary. In his view, his championing of the Bill and his dismissal from office were not unconnected matters, nor was it a coincidence that on his departure responsibility for the Bill was transferred to the Home Secretary.

Speaking in 1997, Justice Michael Kirby welcomed the commitment of the present government to introduce legislation in 1998 but warned against delay. He pointed out that this timetable meant such an Act could not be introduced until eighteen months into the life of the new Parliament and referred to Gareth Evans QC's warning that:

> it was imperative for any government proposing a Freedom of Information Act to get the legislation enacted within the first year of office, lest the skeletons accumulating in the governmental cupboard thereafter render the prospect of enforceable rights of access to information too politically uncongenial to press on with.[72]

We now appreciate that Justice Michael Kirby's optimism about the introduction of the legislation was misplaced; it will not appear until the end of

69 See *Attorney-General for the United Kingdom* v. *Heinmann Publishers Ltd* (1987) 10 N.S.W.L.R. 86
70 *Independent*, 19 November 1998.
71 A. MacKinlay, 319 *H.C. Debs.*, col. 953 (18 November 1998).
72 Kirby, op. cit., n. 40, p. 245, at 249.

1999 at the earliest; no doubt (at that time) the impeding implementation of the Human Rights Act 1998 (and the inevitable consequential bureaucratic and judicial upheaval) will be an excellent excuse for further delaying the Freedom of Information Act.

CONCLUSION

The incorporation of the Convention into the main stream of our common law system has many parallels with the way that the common law absorbed and was invigorated by equity. Convention law can usefully be considered as a 'new equity'.

The incorporation of the Convention into United Kingdom law, whilst welcome, is not in itself a radical step, but more a formalized truce, with the Human Rights Act 1998 spelling out how these new energetic rights will be tolerated within the domestic system.

The Human Rights Act provides the state with a number of politically symbolic benefits and imparts an intellectual rigour to the reform agenda which at times has appeared lacking. It has, however, all the hallmarks of an opiate; it appeases the intellectual 'Charter 88' élite clamouring for constitutional reform and diverts attention from the new government's failure to 'open up the state', and its abandonment of a radical Freedom of Information Act. 'New Labour' has 'gone native'; the Establishment has created a new and subtle ideological discourse ensuring its continued vitality.

85

JOURNAL OF LAW AND SOCIETY
VOLUME 26, NUMBER 1, MARCH 1999
ISSN: 0263-323X, pp. 86-102

The Human Rights Act and Legal Culture:
The Judiciary and the Legal Profession

MURRAY HUNT*

The purpose of this article is to consider the effect the United Kingdom's currently prevailing legal culture is likely to have on the realization of cultural change presaged by the Human Rights Act. The article is in five parts. The first two address the preliminary questions: what is meant by 'legal culture' for these purposes, and what type of 'human rights culture' does the Human Rights Act envisage? The answers define the scope of the remainder of the article's inquiry into the ways in which the Act itself and the culture of the United Kingdom legal profession and judiciary are likely to interact. The third part of the article identifies some examples of the sorts of culturally specific aspects of current legal practice which are likely to operate as serious practical constraints on the emergence of a human rights culture worthy of the name, before the fourth part considers what sorts of cultural changes will be required of judges and lawyers for the presaged cultural transformation to come about. Finally, the article asks whether there is any reason to believe that courts and lawyers can find from within their present culture the resources to bring about the necessary shift.

INTRODUCTION

The passage of the Human Rights Act has been accompanied by much talk of it heralding the long-awaited arrival of a 'human rights culture' in the United Kingdom. Professor Wade, for example, in his 1998 Judicial Studies Board Annual Lecture, sees the Act as 'a quantum leap into a new legal culture of fundamental rights and freedoms'.[1] The Home Secretary, in his speech wrapping up the debate at the end of the Bill's passage through the Commons,

---

1 W. Wade, 'Human Rights and the Judiciary' [1998] *European Human Rights Law Rev.* 520, at 532.

* Barrister, 4-5 Gray's Inn Square, London WC1R 5AY, England

I am grateful to Rabinder Singh and Francesca Klug for their comments.

86

displayed what is probably a more realistic appreciation of the nature of cultural change when he said 'over time, the Bill will bring about the creation of a human rights culture in Britain'.[2] Whatever the time-scale, there seems to be a broad measure of agreement amongst academic commentators, practising lawyers and politicians that the Human Rights Act is a statute of peculiar significance which either represents in its enactment, or has the potential to bring about, change of the order of a cultural transformation.

The overall aim of this article is to arrive at a provisional assessment of how different the present legal culture of the profession and judiciary is from that which will be required in the new human rights culture, with a view to identifying the most likely points of resistance. The importance of law in making human rights effective means that the answers to the questions this article seeks to pose, while by no means the only proper field of inquiry when seeking to assess the Act's prospects of creating such a culture, will nevertheless be important determinants of how soon the government's own vision of a cultural transformation is likely to come about in practice.

THE MEANING OF 'LEGAL CULTURE' FOR PRESENT PURPOSES

There has long been debate between law and society scholars about the meaning and usefulness of the concept of 'legal culture'.[3] This article presupposes the utility of the concept for the purposes of inquiring into the ways in which the various social practices which constitute the legal environment are likely to mediate the concrete effects of the Human Rights Act in practice. On the assumption that this is a worthwhile inquiry, it is proposed to stipulate at the outset a very specific meaning of 'legal culture' for that purpose, and to go on to examine the actual practices of lawyers and judges in the light of that stipulated definition.

An inquiry into the likely dynamic between the Human Rights Act and existing legal culture which takes as its focus the activities of courts and lawyers, as this article does, can do no better than adopt the very helpful definition of legal culture suggested by Karl Klare in his recent account of the transformative potential of rights discourse in South Africa under its new Constitution:[4]

> By legal culture, I mean professional sensibilities, habits of mind, and intellectual reflexes: What are the characteristic rhetorical strategies deployed by participants in a given legal setting? What is their repertoire of recurring argumentative moves? What counts as a persuasive legal argument? What types of arguments, possibly valid in other discursive

2 J. Straw 317 *H.C. Debs.*, col. 1358 (21 October 1998).
3 See, for example, the debate between Roger Cotterrell and Lawrence Friedman in *Comparing Legal Cultures*, ed. D. Nelken (1995) chs. 1 and 2.
4 K. Klare, 'Legal Culture and Transformative Constitutionalism' (1998) 14 *South African J. of Human Rights* 146, at 166–7.

87

contexts (e.g. in political philosophy), are deemed outside the professional discourse of lawyers? What enduring political and ethical commitments influence professional discourse? What understandings of and assumptions about politics, social life and justice? What 'inarticulate premises [are] culturally and historically ingrained'[5] in the professional discourse and outlook?'

That set of questions suffices to define the scope of this article's inquiry into how the legal culture in which lawyers and judges operate is likely to constrain the Act's transformative potential. The object of the inquiry, in short, is to identify those features of the 'complex webs of beliefs, values, understandings and practices'[6] of lawyers and judges which might be at odds with the emergence of a human rights culture.

As a legal practitioner, daily immersed in those social practices, the present writer is not best-placed to transcend the inevitable cultural contingency of the concepts, doctrines, and ways of thinking which constitute legal practice. As Klare rightly reminds us, it is a defining characteristic of legal cultures that its participants often do not perceive the cultural specificity of their ideas about legal argument.[7] The account which follows does not pretend to be written from a perspective external to legal practice, but nevertheless attempts to identify some of the features of current legal practice which are the product of a very particular combination of historical circumstances, many of which have long since ceased to pertain and some of which are now fundamentally challenged by the passage of the Human Rights Act.

Before considering what those features are, however, there is a second preliminary question which will help to shape the inquiry into how far current legal culture is likely to constrain, or be changed by, the different cultural vision thought to be implicit in the Human Rights Act: precisely what type of 'human rights culture' is it envisaged the Act will bring about? The answer to this matters a great deal because what constitutes an obstacle on the journey cannot be recognized until the destination is known.

WHAT TYPE OF 'HUMAN RIGHTS CULTURE'?

Just as there is disagreement as to how soon something of the order of a cultural shift is likely to come about, so also is there likely to be disagreement about the precise nature of the 'human rights culture' which this very particular model of human rights legislation is designed to bring about. Many of those who speak of the advent of a 'human rights culture' will doubtless have in mind a particular conception of such a rights culture, based on the view that the very purpose of a Bill of Rights is to empower the individual citizen against the overbearing, all-powerful state. How widely held this assumption is should not be underestimated: witness, for example, how many

5 *Du Plessis* v. *De Klerk* 1996 (5) BCLR 658 (CC) at para. 119 (Justice Kriegler).
6 Cotterrell in Nelken, op. cit., n. 3, at p. 29.
7 Klare, op. cit., n. 4, at p. 167.

88

of the proliferating articles about the European Convention on Human Rights begin by explaining that it is an instrument designed at the end of the Second World War to prevent fascist states from ever again emerging in Europe. Those who take this view of the nature of the enterprise will envisage a 'human rights culture' in which individuals are transformed from subjects to citizens by endowing them with a set of predominantly negative rights which are to be judicially protected against interference by the state, and the cultural shift thought to be required of courts and the profession to bring about this change will correspond to that purpose. As will be seen in the third part of this article, if this were the type of human rights culture envisaged by the Act, it would be less constrained by our present legal culture, which already has many features of what could be broadly described as a version of liberal legalism.

It is very clear, however, that this is not the conception of a 'human rights culture' which the government and Parliament have sought to bring about by enacting the Human Rights Act. It is clear from the Act's own provisions, from its fundamental scheme and from the various government pronouncements surrounding its enactment, as well as from its place in the wider programme of constitutional reform, that it is designed to introduce a culture of rights that is more communitarian than libertarian in its basic orientation. In such a human rights culture, the individual citizen is more than the mere bearer of negative rights against the state, but is a participative individual, taking an active part in the political realm and accepting the responsibility to respect the rights of others in the community with whom he or she is interdependent. The Human Rights Act introduces a distinctively social-democratic model of human rights protection, combining the protection of individual rights with a role for participative citizens involved in democratic decision-making in their community.[8]

This article is not the place to demonstrate at length the various ways in which the Human Rights Act clearly contemplates such a social-democratic model of rights protection rather than a classical liberal model. For present purposes it will suffice to mention a few of the most significant indicators. One of the most important is the carefully preserved role for democratic decision-makers in the overall scheme. When the Lord Chancellor introduced the Human Rights Bill into the House of Lords, he said that it was designed to 'deliver a modern reconciliation of the inevitable tension between the democratic right of the majority to exercise political power and the democratic need of individuals and minorities to have their rights secured.' This 'modern reconciliation' pervades the entire scheme of the Act, which is designed to institutionalize a creative tension between the judiciary on the one hand and Parliament and the executive on the other. It binds the principal constitutional actors into a dialogue with each other in which all agree

---

8 The origins of the Labour Party's conversion to a Bill of Rights can be traced to Liberty's *A People's Charter* (1991) which demonstrated how rights protection could be balanced with democratic concerns.

89

on the objective of securing Convention rights, and disagreements about their interpretation or the resolution of conflicts between them are mediated by a new relationship between courts and Parliament, both of which have an explicit role in pronouncing on human rights issues. The courts are required to interpret legislation so as to achieve compatibility with the Convention, unless it is linguistically impossible to do so, in which case a declaration of incompatibility must be granted, placing the onus on the executive and Parliament to introduce remedial legislation to remove the incompatibility. There is to be serious pre-legislative scrutiny of all new legislation for conformity with the Convention, ministerial statements of compatibility and a strong parliamentary human rights committee.

The important role accorded to Parliament in the scheme of the Act is an important feature of the government's chosen model for giving effective protection to Convention rights and is a significant indicator of the type of human rights culture which the Act contemplates.[9] A classical liberal scheme of rights protection would be premised on the view of the individual citizen as a bearer of rights enforceable against the state, and would usually be characterized by the judiciary enjoying supremacy over the legislature and the executive in the interpretation of fundamental rights. The government's model, however, is based on a more communitarian notion of the citizen as participative individual, taking an active part in the political realm in which everything is accepted to be the proper object of deliberative action, and there are none of the no-go areas for collective action which liberalism has made it its project to demarcate.

That the government's scheme of rights protection was self-consciously modelled on this more communitarian conception of a human rights culture was made explicit by various spokespersons at different points during the Act's passage. The Home Secretary, in his speech at the end of the Act's passage through the Commons, for example, expressly invoked David Selborne's conception of rights as being inextricable from corresponding responsibilities and duties.[10] In the future development of a human rights culture in the wake of the Act, he called for 'a much clearer understanding among Britain's people and institutions that rights and responsibilities have properly to be balanced – freedoms by obligations and duties'.[11]

Selborne's argument was a reaction against the rights-oriented citizenship of liberalism and an argument for the recognition of mutual duties and responsibilities as the foundation of civic order. Although some versions of the communitarian argument appear to fall for the temptation to invoke the

---

9 For another example of the Act's quite deliberate rejection of a classical liberal model, and explicit preference for a more communitarian or social democratic model, see the express contemplation that the Convention rights will have a degree of horizontal effect, that is, in litigation involving purely private parties (considered further below).

10 D. Selborne, *The Principle of Duty* (1994).

11 J. Straw 317 *H.C. Debs.*, col. 1359 (21 October 1998).

90

community as an excuse for conservative moralizing,[12] there is nothing wrong in principle with this reorientation of the foundations of the liberal project of rights-protection. Indeed, the concept of the participative citizen on which it rests has considerable empowering potential when understood in the context of, for example, Chantal Mouffe's conception of radical democracy, in which individuals are active members of a radical pluralist polity who, through their participation in the many different levels of that polity, achieve greater equality and liberty within their community.[13]

The relevance of such conceptions is clear when the Human Rights Act is considered in the context of the government's much wider programme of constitutional reform. Devolution to parliaments or assemblies in Northern Ireland, Scotland and Wales, the possibility of regional assemblies in England, a representative assembly for London, reform of the House of Lords, freedom of information legislation, and electoral reform are all developments which have the potential at least to contribute to a significant reorientation of the relationship between individuals and their communities, providing them with opportunities to participate in novel ways in decisions affecting them at all different levels of the communities in which they move. When considered in this wider context, it seems clear that the United Kingdom's Human Rights Act is intended to be transformative in a very particular way, as part of a wider programme designed to reinvigorate democracy.

SOME CULTURALLY SPECIFIC ASPECTS OF CURRENT LEGAL PRACTICE

Having now defined the scope and purpose of this article's inquiry, it remains to ask to what extent the prevailing legal culture of the legal profession and judiciary will need to change to accommodate the specific type of human rights culture envisaged, and to what extent that prevailing culture will prevent or hinder the realization of that aspiration. The most cursory consideration of our current legal culture yields a number of examples of habits of mind and patterns of thought on the part of judges and practitioners which are contingent on specific premises and assumptions which may impede the development of the type of human rights culture envisaged by the Act. To describe these as 'culturally specific' or 'contingent' is not to suggest that they may not, in some cases, be a manifestation of underlying concerns which are of a universal nature. It can be readily conceded that often they are motivated by the sorts of concerns which arise in any legal system where

12 A. Etzioni's *The Spirit of Community: Rights, Responsibilities and the Communitarian Agenda* (1995) and *The New Golden Rule* (1997) are particularly susceptible to this criticism. See A. Crawford's review of the former in (1996) 23 *J. of Law and Society* 247.
13 See the interesting use made of Mouffe's conception by Davina Cooper in 'The Citizen's Charter and Radical Democracy: Empowerment and Exclusion within Citizenship Discourse' (1993) 2 *Social and Legal Studies* 149.

constitutional adjudication takes place. Concern about the legitimacy of the role of judges as unelected law-makers, for example, or about how to ensure that due deference is given to democratically accountable decision-makers where it is warranted, are ever-present dilemmas in any system where courts exercise a judicial review function over the executive and administration. In what follows in this part, what is meant by a particular assumption, technique, method or practice being culturally specific is merely that it is at least in part the product of a particular set of historical circumstances which have shaped legal practice by giving rise to accepted norms and ways of reasoning and arguing which have been internalized by the principal actors in the legal system, the judges and the lawyers. Acceptance that the ground-rules of legal practice are, at least to this degree, contingent is the first important step to re-examining those practices in the light of what is now required by the Human Rights Act.

At the risk of over-simplification, there is some justification for saying that there are two particular features of this country's currently prevailing legal culture that are most likely to hinder the development of the human rights culture envisaged by the Human Rights Act. One is the unquestioning loyalty demanded to the absolute, continuing, and indivisible sovereignty of Parliament and the other is the acceptance of the primacy of private ordering. These are the twin foundations of our constitutional arrangements which we have inherited from Dicey. Their influence is all-pervasive: virtually everything in our present legal culture which threatens to be inimical to the development of the sort of human rights culture envisaged can be traced back to these two premises. They condition what courts and lawyers consider to count as 'legal' arguments and they dictate a very particular mindset which subscribes wholeheartedly to the view that the courts are merely neutral arbiters applying 'legal' rules and principles which never embroils them in controversial value choices which might threaten their legitimacy.

I have sought to challenge each of the Diceyan premises elsewhere, questioning the more extravagant claims of sovereignty theory and in particular the unnecessary obstacles it has erected to the reception of human rights law and values,[14] and arguing that so long as priority is given to private ordering, constitutionalism will continue to be concerned primarily with the protection of private law values such as property rather than more public values.[15] The argument is that each of the Diceyan premises has the capacity to threaten to prevent the long overdue modernization of constitutional practice. For the purposes of this article, however, I merely want to identify some of the concrete ways in which those bedrock assumptions manifest themselves in daily legal practice to demonstrate how rooted is our present legal culture in a paradigm which in many ways is fundamentally at odds with the type of human rights culture that the Human Rights Act foreshadows.

14 M. Hunt, *Using Human Rights Law in English Courts* (1997).
15 See M. Hunt, 'Constitutionalism and the Contractualisation of Government in the UK' in *The Province of Administrative Law*, ed. M. Taggart (1997) and 'The "Horizontal Effect" of the Human Rights Act' [1998] *Public Law* 423.

The most obvious manifestation of these unspoken cultural commitments are to be found in the techniques and methodologies of legal interpretation and adjudication. Despite undoubted progress in recent years, largely under the influence of a small number of particularly influential judges, the prevailing legal culture remains firmly attached to highly traditional methods of legal analysis. It is often highly formalistic, preferring to take refuge in the familiarity of well-known rules and interpretive approaches than to engage with the illuminating debates which have long been emanating from the legal academy challenging received views about the determinacy of legal texts and the contingency of meaning. Statutory interpretation may have moved on from the worst formalistic excesses of the days when the literalist school prevailed, but even the comparatively recent embrace of 'purposive' interpretation, most notably in the decision in *Pepper* v. *Hart* permitting reference to *Hansard* as an interpretive aid,[16] is decidedly positivistic in its assumption that there is in every legislative text an actual meaning with a real existence as a historical fact which can be uncovered with the necessary tools, rather than a putative meaning that needs to be constructed by reference to a range of different legally relevant materials. The attraction of characterising the enterprise in the former way, of course, is to minimize the amount of value-choice involved in performing the judicial function, and thereby to avoid the awkward questions of the legitimacy of judges making value choices for which they cannot readily be called to account. This is the strategic move which Klare accurately labels 'depoliticising the rule of law'.

Much the same can be said of the prevailing judicial techniques and methodologies in interpreting non-statutory legal rules. Again, the days when courts pretended that they 'discovered' the common law, in the way scorned by Lord Reid in his famous essay as long ago as 1972,[17] may be gone, but that powerful judicial instinct to evade responsibility for making law has not. By and large our judges rarely say explicitly that they are 'developing' the common law. More often than not a significant common law development will need to be unearthed by scholars from what purports to be merely an application of existing law to a new set of facts. When courts are directly confronted by an invitation to develop the common law explicitly, in a way which could not be concealed, they are likely to consider it to be an illegitimate exercise in judicial law-making.[18]

Closely allied to the traditional judicial reluctance to be candid about the inevitable scope for value-choice in legal interpretation is the narrowness of

16 [1993] A.C. 593.
17 J. Reid, 'The Judge as Law Maker' (1972) *12 J. of Society of Public Teachers of Law* 22.
18 See, for example, *Hunter* v. *Canary Wharf* [1997] 2 W.L.R. 684, in which the House of Lords declined to develop the common law of private nuisance, insisting that it remained necessary to have an interest in property to be able to bring such an action. A good example of the significance of different cultural assumptions about law can be gained from comparing the majority's view with that of Lord Cooke from New Zealand, who did not feel so constrained (see 713H–714A).

the prevailing view of the nature of the judicial function, even in judicial review cases in which the judiciary most explicitly sits in judgment over decision-makers who often have a far better democratic pedigree. Fearful of being drawn into debates over deeply contested issues of morality or public policy, the courts frequently take refuge in a series of doctrinal devices designed to insulate them from the criticism that they are merely giving effect to their subjective preferences. The distinctions to which courts frequently resort, between review and appeal, legality and the merits, process and substance, law and 'policy', are all examples of such judicial self-protection, as are more substantive 'doctrines' such as the high Wednesbury standard of review. There is also explicit acceptance of legitimating fictions, such as the doctrine of *ultra vires* and the entire doctrinal edifice which rests upon it, which are accepted by many as necessary evils in order to protect the courts against the loss of their legitimacy.[19] Many of these are attempts to give effect to genuine and entirely proper concerns about the limits to the legitimacy of the judicial role, but in the manner of all doctrines they have taken on a life of their own. They often appear disconnected from their original rationale, or unnecessarily blunt instruments which go far further than is necessary to avoid the perceived loss of legitimacy to which a particular argument appears inevitably to lead.

Yet another manifestation of the sorts of unarticulated cultural premises underlying legal practice is the continued vitality in United Kingdom legal culture of a firm distinction between public and private, and a clear orientation towards the private as the proper sphere of judicial activity. This particular construct can be directly traced to Dicey's very particular account of the rule of law in terms of the primacy of the individual's private rights as recognized and protected by the courts in private law. The legacy of that account is that principles of interpretation are made up largely of presumptions in favour of a certain set of values which are private in nature, and in particular property-based, and are assumed to be 'neutral' in that they reflect some pre-political state of nature before the state began to intervene in private matters.

The traditional primacy of private ordering also means that the private law model of adjudication, involving a bipolar dispute between two parties about the extent of their rights and duties, is considered to be the 'normal' model within which adjudication should take place. This has profound implications for the applicable procedural rules, concerning matters such as costs, standing, interventions, and what evidence is admissible. It also predisposes courts towards an assumption that social and economic rights, or any claims on the state which may involve the performance of a positive duty involving public expenditure, are on the whole not justiciable, because they cannot be fitted very easily into the private law forms and methods of adjudication.

19 See, for example, C. Forsyth, 'Of Fig Leafs and Fairy Tales' (1996) 55 *Cambridge Law J.* 122.

94

The individualistic focus of the private law suit tends to obscure the wider issues which are often at stake in litigation involving human rights. As Ireland and Laleng have observed:

> law in its construction of issues marginalises certain experiences and voices, and . . . when problems are (re-)defined in legal terms, the social structures and processes of which they are part often disappear from view. Crucially, of course, when such structures and processes are overlooked, so too are vitally important questions of power.[20]

These various habits of mind amongst judges in their approach to performing their task of adjudicating find their echo in the legal profession itself, which, like any profession, is a very reliable vehicle for the transmission of cultural values and thus the perpetuation of the prevailing ways of thinking and doing. Quite apart from any vested class interest which many members of the legal profession might well have in preserving the prevailing culture,[21] there are a number of different pressures at work on practising lawyers which constrain the extent to which challenges to the prevailing culture are likely to be made. Often these are straightforward practical constraints. Inevitably, the judicial habits of mind described above to a large degree set the parameters of legal argument and define the limits to the sorts of arguments and evidence that practitioners consider it to be worthwhile investing time and resources in preparing. It is pointless wasting time and energy preparing a thoroughly researched and reasoned argument when the prospect of appearing before a judge who will consider it to be a valid argument at all, let alone a *good* valid argument, may be slim. Moreover, there is also a very real funding constraint. Litigants who are not well served by the prevailing legal culture are nearly always publicly funded, which imposes an onerous responsibility on representatives to confine their arguments to those with a realistic prospect of success. Legal aid is not available to test the limits of cultural change. The judicial resistance to the relevance of certain types of argument therefore becomes self-fulfilling for a number of practical reasons.

In addition, there are powerful informal pressures on lawyers to conform to the prevailing culture. It is a peculiar feature of this country's positivist tradition that it is often defended with a zeal of which Dicey himself would have been proud. Many of the culturally specific aspects of legal practice which have been identified above have acquired the status of articles of faith, making comparisons between judges and lawyers on the one hand and the priesthood on the other not entirely unfair.[22] A practising lawyer's vocational training is the beginning of a lengthy process of socialization into a professional culture with very clear, and very particular, ideas about the nature of legal argumentation. The sanction for perceived infidelity to a 'canon' of interpretation, or

20 P. Ireland and P. Laleng, 'Critical Legal Studies and Radical Politics' in *The Critical Lawyers' Handbook* 2, eds. P. Ireland and P. Laleng (1997) 2.
21 Of which the most vivid and readable account remains J.A.G. Griffith's *The Politics of the Judiciary* (5th edn., 1997).
22 See, for example, P. Fitzpatrick, *The Mythology of Modern Law* (1992).

for venturing an argument which might not be thought to qualify as 'legal', may be no greater than the whisperings of fellow professionals about whether that individual is a 'good lawyer', or it may be a public rebuke from the bench.

More serious consequences could even potentially follow if the lawyer is perceived by the relevant professional bodies to have infringed a professional rule of conduct as a result of a conscientiously held view of the nature of law and legal argument. To subscribe to a non-positivist conception of law, for example, opens up the possibility of disagreement over what counts as a 'legal' argument, the implications of which for the Bar's so-called 'cab-rank rule' have yet to be tested. The professional codes of conduct, like law itself, are not neutral rules of uncontroversial content. They are as much the product of the prevailing legal culture as the practices described above. They too are derived from a model of adjudication based largely on the private law paradigm of adversarial adjudication and positivist assumptions about what counts as law. There is a steadily growing literature exploring the connection between particular rules of professional conduct and the underlying view of law and adjudication.[23] It would be surprising if a shift in culture of the type under discussion here did not cause some points of tension with rules of professional conduct based on premises which become increasingly contested as the nature of the legal system changes.

WHAT CHANGES IN LEGAL CULTURE WILL BE REQUIRED?

This account of the potential obstacles inherent in our present legal culture brings us to consider the changes in legal culture which will be required if the type of human rights culture it is intended to promote is to be realized. Some of these changes are required very directly by the actual text of the Human Rights Act, while others are more implicit in its general scheme or appear from the wider context of constitutional reform of which the enactment of the Human Rights Act forms a part. Still others can be identified which will be necessary in the longer term for the culture truly to take root in the domestic legal system and to acquire the status of a commitment to constitutionalism which is not vulnerable to short-term political changes.

The first and most explicit cultural change required, and potentially one of the most far-reaching, is to the traditional techniques of statutory interpretation. This change is mandated explicitly in the actual terms of the Act, section 3 imposing on all interpreters of legislation (primary and subordinate,

---

23 See, for example. P.G. Haskell, *Why Lawyers Behave As They Do* (1998) and W.H. Simon, *The Practice of Justice: A Theory of Lawyers' Ethics* (1998). The latter rejects the 'dominant view' of legal ethics that lawyers' primary duty is to pursue their client's interests zealously within the bounds of the law, in favour of what he calls the 'contextual view', founded on lawyers' self-professed moral aspiration to be part of a justice-seeking profession. According to Simon's contextual view, lawyers' ethical duties cannot be wholly separated from the underlying merits of a case.

96

past and future) an interpretive obligation, namely to interpret the legislation in a way which is compatible with Convention rights, 'so far as it is possible to do so'. This represents an important departure from more traditional techniques, described above, in which courts and tribunals have applied well-established rules and principles of interpretation to ascertain what was actually 'meant' by the particular Parliament which enacted the legislation in question. The nature of the enterprise is no longer the excavation of some historical meaning, but an exercise in constructing meaning from different legal sources, subject only to the overriding constraint that the legislative words cannot be given a meaning that linguistically they cannot bear. Section 3 does not require the courts to interpret black to mean white. In such a case the only course open to the court is to grant a declaration of incompatibility.

The intended effect of s. 3 is quite unequivocal. It explicitly requires courts to use their interpretive ingenuity to avoid an incompatibility with Convention rights. Moreover, by making a declaration of incompatibility available in cases where a compatible interpretation is not possible, the scheme of the Act cleverly binds courts into a scheme which gives them every incentive to discover the interpretive flexibility to avoid granting such declarations. This makes them likely to reach compatible interpretations which they might not otherwise have reached by more traditional interpretive techniques. As the White Paper makes clear, the interpretive obligation imposed by s. 3 goes far beyond merely taking the Convention into account in resolving ambiguity in legislation.[24]

Yet, despite the clarity of the provision itself, and the unequivocal statement of purpose as to what it is supposed to achieve, there are already clear indications of the way in which even a provision explicitly mandating a change of methodology is capable of being assimilated and effectively neutralized by the prevailing legal culture, if it is understood, not as a transformative provision in its own right, but in terms of the very culture in reaction to which it is being introduced. A debate has broken out about the meaning of the words 'so far as it is possible to do so' in s. 3. Marshall, in a fine example of the prevailing culture's refusal to countenance legal change on anything other than its own terms, has suggested that, in effect, it means so far as it can be done within existing rules and principles of statutory interpretation.[25] On this view, courts would not be able to 'stretch' or 'distort' the language of statutes, or depart from their plain meaning when this has been long settled. In similar fashion, Wade has said that by s. 3, 'the judges are given a new task, to interpret *uncertain or ambiguous provisions* not according to what they think is the true meaning, but according to the meaning which best accords with the Convention rights'.[26] Such arguments mischaracterize the nature of the new interpretive obligation, which

24 Home Office, *Rights Brought Home: The Human Rights Bill* (1997; Cm. 3782) at para. 2.7.
25 G. Marshall, 'Interpreting Interpretation in the Human Rights Bill' [1998] *Public Law* 167.
26 W. Wade, 'The United Kingdom's Bill of Rights', in *Constitutional Reform in the United Kingdom: Practice and Principles* (1998) at 66 (emphasis added).

is clearly based on the strong Marleasing obligation in European Community law, according to which a compatible interpretation must be reached unless the language of the provision makes such an interpretation impossible. Nevertheless, the Wade/Marshall view might well find favour with constitutionally conservative judges who remain wedded to the old assumptions about the nature of statutory interpretation.

The assimilationist tendency of the prevailing culture ought not to be underestimated. A good example is the way in which practitioners' texts explain the significance of recent legal developments for busy practitioners with too little time to reflect on them. In the 1992 edition of the practitioner's bible on statutory interpretation, Bennion's *Statutory Interpretation: A Code*, for example, the status of fundamental rights had become such as to merit inclusion in part XVII of the author's *Code of Interpretation*, as part of a wider general principle 'against doubtful penalisation'. In other words, the recent enthusiasm of some judges for construing statutes against a background presumption in favour of fundamental rights is explained as just one more manifestation of the well-established technique of construing the language of statutes strictly so as to minimize the extent to which they interfere with values such as property or personal liberty. Such is the power of the prevailing categories of thought that no development is sufficiently fundamental or significant that it cannot be fitted neatly within those categories, with the minimum of disturbance to the underlying premises about what law is and what legal actors do.

The new interpretive obligation will require another profound cultural change, in that it will require courts and tribunals to ignore the doctrine of precedent where an earlier interpretation of a legislative provision by a higher court was not arrived at after asking whether such an interpretation was compatible with Convention rights. Although this is not spelt out in terms in the Act, it follows from the unequivocal terms of the obligation in s. 3: once the Act comes into effect, every court and tribunal will be required to reach interpretations of legislation which are compatible with Convention rights. To the extent that any previous interpretation is incompatible with the Convention, the new interpretive obligation requires them to prefer the new, compatible interpretation. The White Paper spells out this consequence more explicitly, making clear that courts and tribunals will not be bound by previous interpretations of existing legislation, even by higher courts.[27]

Two other changes to judges' and lawyers' interpretive techniques and methodologies will also be required, although, as with the derogation from the doctrine of precedent, these are implicit in the Act's scheme rather than explicitly required in the way that s. 3 explicitly requires a particular approach

---

27 op. cit., n. 24, para. 2.8. Notwithstanding the clarity of the text and the explicit intention, the resilience of the prevailing culture makes it possible that the Marshall view about the meaning of 'so far as it is possible to do so' may also be relied on to persuade a court that s. 3 cannot require disregard of a higher court's interpretation, because that is not 'possible' under the doctrine of precedent.

98

to statutory interpretation. First, as the White Paper again points out, courts will have to bear in mind that the Convention is a 'living instrument' to be interpreted in the light of present day conditions to reflect changing social attitudes. Such a dynamic, evolutionary approach to interpretation is quite at odds with the much more conservative interpretive tradition of United Kingdom judges as described above. Second, the fact that courts and tribunals are themselves 'public authorities' for the purposes of the Act, and therefore obliged to act compatibly with the Convention, means that they will also have to shed their reluctance to develop the common law where it is necessary to do so in order to achieve compatibility with the Convention. Resistance to some doctrinal fluidity in private law will therefore also have to change.

Another important change required by the Act which goes against the grain of the prevailing legal culture is the inevitable expansion of the judicial function which will be involved in cases where what is alleged is a breach by a public authority of a Convention right. Section 6(1) of the Act makes it unlawful for a public authority to act in a way which is incompatible with Convention rights. The clarity of that obligation leaves no room for any doubt that the courts are going to have to carry out the very proportionality exercise which they have for so long feared is inconsistent with the legitimacy of their role. The very nature of the adjudicative function will inevitably be transformed in such cases. The court will have to carry out a highly structured exercise in judicial reasoning identical to that carried out by the Court in Strasbourg. They will have to decide whether the interest for which protection is sought is within the scope of a Convention right, whether there has been an interference with that right, whether that interference is prescribed by law, whether it serves a legitimate aim, whether it corresponds to a pressing social need, and whether the extent of the interference is proportionate to the aim pursued. As the White Paper again makes clear, courts will be required to balance the protection of individuals' fundamental rights against the demands of the general interest of the community. Judges will therefore be forced to overcome their narrow view of the forms and limits of adjudication.[28]

With this expansion of the legitimate judicial role, it is to be hoped that the courts will embrace a more explicit acknowledgment of the irreducible political content of adjudication. Judges, and therefore lawyers, should feel liberated by the Act from their obsessive concern about the legitimacy of their judicial review function. The Human Rights Act is the most explicit legislative endorsement of that role ever to have emanated from Parliament,

---

28 With this expansion of the judicial role in adjudicating on matters of morality, the range of materials to be regarded as legally relevant will also have to expand, to include, for example, greater use of comparative material and of academic literature, including philosophical literature. As Lord Steyn has observed, instead of a thousand dicta on the concept of Wednesbury unreasonableness, 'it may be more helpful to dip into Isaiah Berlin' ([1998] *European Human Rights Law Rev.* 153 at 156).

99

and it has the added legitimacy of having been an explicit manifesto commitment, not only of the political party which won an overwhelming majority
in the Commons, but of the political parties who between them commanded
the support of about two-thirds of those voting. By the same token, it is
also to be hoped that judges, with the assistance of respondents' lawyers,
will begin to articulate their reasons why deference in a particular case may
be warranted, instead of reaching for the crude instruments of Wednesbury
unreasonableness, Parliamentary sovereignty, or the over-used distinctions
between appeal/merits, law/politics or procedure/substance. In this respect,
the Human Rights Act is an unprecedented opportunity for courts to
enhance the legitimacy of their role in the protection of human rights and
to delimit it in a more sensitive and explicit way than historically has been
felt possible.[29]

One further cultural change that will be required is an acceptance of a
degree of horizontality in the application of Convention rights. The model
which has been chosen to give effect to Convention rights very deliberately
seeks to make them all-pervasive, with the result that their effects will be felt
in a wide range of proceedings before courts and tribunals, including in
proceedings between purely private parties. The degree of horizontal application which the government have in mind was explained by the Lord
Chancellor during the debates in the House of Lords, where he said that it
was thought right as a matter of principle that the courts ought to be under
the duty to act compatibly with the Convention when developing the
common law in deciding cases between individuals.[30] This important feature
of the Act, which is one of the respects in which the Act is more in the nature
of a social democratic than a classical liberal Bill of Rights, will require a
reconsideration of the public/private distinction in the prevailing culture.[31]

CONCLUSION

The changes which are required of the judiciary and legal profession in order
to bring about the type of human rights culture envisaged by the Human

29 A heavy onus of responsibility for broadening judicial horizons also rests on practitioners.
   As Sedley J. has observed, 'how much the judicial mindset changes in relation to human
   rights is going to depend to an unusual degree on the quality of analysis and presentation
   of a legal profession whose minds are perhaps fresher and more innovative than those of
   their elders': see 'Human Rights: A New Dawn or an Old Dilemma?' [1998] 1 *Queen Mary
   and Westfield Law J.* 15, at 16.
30 583 *H.L. Debs.*, col. 783 (24 November 1997).
31 Many other changes of a more systemic kind will also become necessary in the longer term.
   For example, the system for appointment of the judiciary will inevitably come under much
   more scrutiny than at present as a result of the greater importance of the judicial function
   under the Act, and the need for an appropriately diverse judiciary will become even more
   urgent. As noted above, the implications for professional codes of conduct also remain to
   be worked out. The absence of any women or ethnic minorities on the United Kingdom's
   highest court will be simply unacceptable.

100

Rights Act are therefore considerable if the currently prevailing legal culture is not to act as a strong brake on progress towards that position. Is there any reason to suppose that practitioners and judges can find within their current resources the means to bring about the necessary transformation?

Although the picture painted above was of a prevailing legal culture which does not provide a promising seedbed in which a human rights culture could easily take root, present practice is not as monolithic as that picture might suggest. In some respects contemporary legal practice is in a state of flux, and a number of developments in recent years give cause for optimism that the necessary transformation can be brought about by accelerating certain trends and hastening the demise of outmoded ways of thinking. The most obvious example of such a development, although it has been slow in coming, is the constitutional accommodation of European Community law. Over the last twenty-five years, courts and tribunals have developed a more flexible approach to the interpretation of domestic legislation in order to fulfil the obligations of membership. In the early years, courts discovered a new interpretive flexibility in order to avoid having to find an incompatibility between an Act of Parliament and directly effective, and therefore supreme, Community law. More recently, courts have embraced a similar flexibility in the interpretation of domestic legislation so as to be compatible with non-directly effective Community law. European Community membership has also been the catalyst for a greater receptiveness into English law of 'European' legal concepts such as legitimate expectation and proportionality. Not many years ago these had no place in our legal lexicon, but, under the increasingly pervasive influence of European Community law, our judiciary has become steadily more receptive to such ideas and concepts from other legal systems.

Finally, and probably the most significant portent of the prospects of developing an indigenous human rights culture, there has very recently emerged what can only be called a common law human rights jurisdiction. Since about the turn of the present decade, courts have fashioned from the common law a variety of ways of according a greater degree of protection to fundamental rights. In some cases, they have moulded a strong presumption of statutory interpretation, that Parliament does not intend to legislate inconsistently with fundamental rights and freedoms. In others they have refined the common law of judicial review by applying a more exacting standard of review to decisions which interfere with fundamental rights. In yet other cases, courts have asserted an identity between the common law and the Convention and occasionally have actively developed the common law so as to achieve such an identity. In addition, courts have often been scrupulous to ensure that judicial discretions are exercised compatibly with the Convention. Moreover, a number of these significant developments have taken place in private litigation in which the courts have considered themselves to be bound to interpret the common law governing private disputes in a way which avoids violation of Convention rights, thus according a degree of horizontal effect to such rights even before the Act comes into effect.

101

If the present generation of judges and lawyers are to transform these existing elements of legal culture into the fully-fledged changes of approach described above as necessary, they will need to acquire a habit for critical self-reflection on their roles and techniques. This will require them to show a new sense of humility and critical inquiry, qualities for which, with some notable exceptions, they have not hitherto been renowned. It demands an open-mindedness, a receptiveness to new ideas, a willingness to reappraise long-held convictions and assumptions about the nature of law and legal practice, and to shed those reflexive techniques and methodologies which are no longer appropriate. Above all they will need to be alert to the ability of the prevailing legal culture to absorb change by an invisible assimilative process.

The only guarantee against such assimilation is for judges and lawyers to remain acutely aware that the Human Rights Act must be seen, not as just another statute to be interpreted as any other, but as part of a much wider programme of constitutional change designed to reinvigorate democracy. Northern Ireland apart, Britain has been fortunate that its Human Rights Act is not the product of the painful transformation and political upheaval that preceded the adoption of such instruments in countries such as South Africa. But just as those instruments are to be interpreted in light of their self-consciously transformative purpose in introducing a new democratic order, so the Human Rights Act must be seen as part of a wider programme of constitutional reform. The present government, with the support of other political parties, is itself engaged on its own process of transformative constitutionalism. It may not be as momentous as the transformations that have taken place elsewhere, but that only makes it all the more important for courts and lawyers to acquire a heightened sense of critical consciousness of what is required to change. Highly stable prevailing or dominant cultures, which after all comprise only the understandings, beliefs, instincts, and fears of human actors, have a tendency to absorb new changes into their familiar ways and habits. If that is not to be the fate of the Human Rights Act, judges and practitioners must constantly remind themselves that the Act is no ordinary piece of legislation, to be interpreted like the rest, but is part of a much wider programme of constitutional reform designed to bring about democratic renewal of the country's institutions.

JOURNAL OF LAW AND SOCIETY
VOLUME 26, NUMBER 1, MARCH 1999
ISSN: 0263-323X, pp. 103-27

The Third Way in Mental Health Policy: Negative Rights, Positive Rights, and the Convention

PHILIP FENNELL*

Mentally disordered patients may be said to have rights in two senses: negative rights to freedom from arbitrary detention or interference with their person; and positive rights to expect a certain minimum standard of service, be that in terms of treatment as an in-patient, or as a patient in the community. The Labour government has appointed a 'scoping group' to carry out a root-and-branch review of the Mental Health Act 1983. The 1983 Act was mainly concerned with in-patient treatment. The group is to look at the scope for introducing further compulsory powers in the community, enhancing the rights of carers and relatives, and is to take account of recent British and Strasbourg case law. The primary impact of the Convention on psychiatric patients has been in relation to protection against arbitrary detention under Article 5, unsoundness of mind being one of the permitted grounds of deprivation of liberty under Article 5(1)(e). This article explores the potential impact of Convention rights in developing what Gostin referred to in the early 1980s as a 'new legalism'. The new legalism linked concern for traditional rights to due process and review by the courts or other external bodies with the 'ideology of entitlement' to adequate treatment and services. The article outlines the current policy context of mental health services and looks at the development by the European Court of Human Rights of positive Convention rights to services out of Article 5, whose purpose seems at first sight to be the protection of due process rights. It examines the relevance of Convention rights to community powers.[1]

---

1 For reasons of space, this article will not survey all the implications of Convention rights for English mental health law. For a very useful summary, see O. Thorold, 'The Implications of the European Convention on Human Rights for United Kingdom Mental Health Legislation' [1996] *European Human Rights Law Rev.* 619–36. See, also, M.C. Wachenfeld, *The Human Rights of the Mentally Ill in Europe under the European Convention on Human Rights* (1992).

* Reader in Law, Cardiff Law School, P.O Box 427, Museum Avenue, Cardiff CF1 1XD, Wales

103

© Blackwell Publishers Ltd 1999, 108 Cowley Road, Oxford OX4 1JF, UK and 350 Main Street, Malden, MA 02148, USA

INTRODUCTION: HUMAN RIGHTS AND MENTAL HEALTH POLICY

In July 1998 the Secretary of State for Health, Frank Dobson, declared that community care had failed. He wanted 'a third way' in mental health.[2] The third way would steer a path between reliance on putting all mentally ill people in institutions – 'out of sight – out of mind' – and community care where people with mental health problems could be 'left off the books' thereby putting themselves and other people at risk. The third way is not greatly different from the policy proclaimed by Stephen Dorrell in the last years of John Major's Conservative government, replacing community care by 'spectrum of care'.[3] Like spectrum of care, the third way involves developing a range of services, ranging from the top-security special hospitals, which provide care for patients with dangerous or violent proclivities, through to community provision. This would include:

> specialist regional secure units in every NHS Region; accommodation in every locality to provide short-term round the clock nursing care and supervision; assertive outreach teams to keep tabs on people who have been discharged and make contact with people who shy away from getting help; and changes to enable carers and professionals to respond promptly and effectively to the needs of mentally ill patients in the community.

The 'third way' included a promise of 'root and branch review' of mental health law 'to reflect the opportunities and limits of modern therapies and drugs'. 'It will cover such possible measures as compliance orders and community treatment orders to provide a prompt and effective legal basis to ensure that patients get supervised care if they do not take their medication and their condition deteriorates.'[4] The Secretary of State subsequently appointed a 'scoping' group chaired by Professor Genevra Richardson to consider reform of the Mental Health Act 1983. The 1983 Act consolidated the Mental Health (Amendment) Act 1982 and the Mental Health Act 1959, and has since been amended by the Mental Health (Patients in the Community) Act 1995.

The 1959 Act reflected a 'medicalist' orientation, conferring on mental health professionals wide discretionary powers to detain and, it was assumed, to treat compulsorily.[5] Although built on the essentially discretionary foundation of the 1959 Act, the 1983 Act reflects a much stronger rights orientation than its

2 Whilst the last years of the Conservative government were characterized by the packaging of policy in terms of point-plans (usually ten-point plans), the policy mantra of the Blair government has been 'the third way.'

3 HSG(96)6\LASSL (96)6, *The Spectrum of Care – A summary of comprehensive local services for people with mental health problems*, and the NHS Patient's Charter for Mental Health Services (NHS Executive EL(97)1).

4 Department of Health press release 98/311 29 July 1998.

5 For a fuller discussion of medicalism and the competing philosophy of legalism see P. Fennell, 'Law and Psychiatry' in *Legal Frontiers*, ed. P.A. Thomas (1996) 208–64. It provides under one legislative umbrella for the detention of both non-offender and offender patients.

predecessor, following as it did upon an intensive reform campaign by MIND (the National Association for Mental Health) and its legal officer Larry Gostin, a campaign which included the bringing of a number of test cases before the European Commission and Court of Human Rights. Gostin described the 1983 Act as embodying a 'new legalism'. The new legalism not only seeks to protect traditional 'negative' rights in the sense of freedom from arbitrary and unjustified detention, and the right to external review of psychiatric decision-making. It builds on traditional rights-based approaches by emphasizing entitlement to care in the least restrictive alternative setting – the ideology of entitlement – that sufferers have the right to an adequate service.[6]

Many provisions of the 1983 Act were introduced to bring the United Kingdom into compliance with the Convention. The 1982 amendments were to a large extent a recognition of what the Strasbourg court has since referred to as 'the particular situation of inferiority and powerlessness which is typical of patients confined in psychiatric hospitals'.[7] They were inspired by a desire to ensure that patients detained in hospital had frequent rights to review of their detention by independent tribunals (mental health review tribunals – MHRTs), as well as to review of decisions to treat without consent. Part IV of the 1983 Act makes explicit for the first time the power to treat without consent, but recognizes the controversial nature of psychotropic medication and electroconvulsive therapy by requiring an independent second opinion if they are to be given without consent. Part IV also prohibits psychosurgery without valid consent. Finally, following a large number of reports of inquiries into abuses in psychiatric hospitals, a new special health authority, the Mental Health Act Commission (MHAC), was given general oversight of the treatment of detained patients and the power to investigate their complaints. Concerns about possible infringement of the right of access to a court in determination of civil rights and liabilities Article 6 lay behind a relaxation of the restriction on bringing legal actions against people acting pursuant to mental health legislation.

The most significant of the test cases brought by MIND in terms of impact on legislation was the 1981 decision of the European Court in *X. v. United Kingdom*[8] that all persons detained on grounds of unsoundness of mind are entitled under Article 5(4) to seek review at periodic intervals of the lawfulness of their detention by a court, which must have the power to order discharge. The ruling led to significant increases in the role of mental health review tribunals, set up under the Mental Health Act 1959 to review the continued need for psychiatric detention. The 1983 Act increased the frequency of patients' entitlement to seek review of their case by a tribunal and gave them new powers to discharge patients detained for up to twenty-eight days' assessment, who had previously enjoyed no tribunal rights.

6 L.O. Gostin, 'Perspectives on Mental Health Reforms' (1983) 10 *J. of Law and Society* 47–70.
7 *Herczegfalvy* v. *Austria* (1992) 18 *Butterworths Medico-Legal Reports* 48.
8 *X* v. *United Kingdom* (1981) 4 *European Human Rights Reports* 188; (1981) 1 *Butterworths Medico-Legal Reports* 98.

Offender patients sentenced to hospital orders with restriction orders because of their dangerousness ('restriction-order patients') were given the right to apply to the tribunal, and the tribunal was given powers to order their discharge. Previously the tribunals' function with restriction-order patients had been limited to giving advice on the patient's suitability for discharge to the Home Secretary, who was free to reject their advice. Automatic hearings were introduced for patients who do not apply to the tribunal within a specified period of detention.

The 1983 Act reflects patient entitlement to treatment in the least restrictive setting in the admission and renewal criteria by making it a condition of detention for treatment that it is certified that treatment cannot be provided without resort to compulsory admission. But for treatment in less restrictive community settings to work effectively, community care services are needed. The one provision of the 1983 Act to reflect positive rights in terms of entitlement to services is s. 117. It puts a joint duty on the local health authority and the local social services authority to provide, in co-operation with relevant voluntary agencies, aftercare services for patients who have been detained under long-term powers of detention, until the authorities are satisfied that they no longer need them. This entitlement to services was later supplemented by an obligation to accept those services (especially drug treatment) under the Mental Health (Patients in the Community) Act 1995.

The 1995 Act marks the shift in focus of mental health policy, evident by the early 1990s, away from the vulnerability of psychiatric in-patients towards responding to the potential dangerousness of patients in the community. Many of the large psychiatric hospitals where the scandals of the 1960s, 1970s, and early 1980s took place have now closed or are in the process of closure, to be replaced by smaller units, and patients are being increasingly cared for in the community. Homicides by psychiatric patients must be followed by an inquiry and inquiry reports invariably highlight poor community care of discharged psychiatric patients. Whilst the inquiries of the 1970s and 1980s concerned abuses in institutions, those of the 1990s have concerned decisions to discharge and failures in community care of patients who subsequently commit homicide. Despite the fact that fear of homicides by psychiatric patients has become the primary engine of mental health policy, research by Gunn and Taylor shows that homicides by mentally disordered people have steadily fallen since the 1950s.[9]

The image of psychiatric patients which lay behind the new legalism and which dominated the agenda in the 1980s was of detainees in institutions suffering abuse because of lack of rights to external review of their detention and treatment, and inadequate community support to enable those who could to survive outside hospital. Failure to make adequate community provision for patients who had been in hospital, and poor co-ordination of

9 D. Brindle, 'Killings by mentally ill are falling' *Guardian*, 6 January 1999, 4.

106

community care services during the late 1980s were to lead by the early 1990s to new images of mentally disordered people as threats to public safety. In 1992 the newly appointed Conservative Secretary of State for Health, Virginia Bottomley, expressed the view that the 'pendulum' had swung too far in the direction of civil liberties. The Care Programme Approach, introduced in 1990, required a key worker and a care plan for every patient discharged by the specialist psychiatric services.[10] From 1993 onwards, the Conservative government introduced a raft of measures designed to require patients to accept medicine in the community.[11]

By the mid-1990s the perception was firmly entrenched that psychiatric patients were endangering themselves and others precisely because they had 'too many rights'. By this was meant that once patients left hospital, the possibilities of requiring them to continue with their medication were limited, leading to a 'revolving door' whereby patients cease to take their medication not long after leaving hospital, become steadily worse, and eventually require re-admission on section, to be discharged only for the cycle to repeat itself. Until the mid-1980s, psychiatrists used a device rather offensively referred to as 'the long leash'[12] to require discharged patients to continue with their medication on a long-term basis. This was declared unlawful by McCullough J. in *R.* v. *Hallstrom ex parte W (No 2)*.[13]

The 'long leash' meant that patients were never effectively discharged. Instead they would be sent on leave, a condition of their leave being that they continue taking medication. The hospital psychiatrist could recall the patient to hospital by giving an order in writing if she or he considered it necessary in the interests of the patient's health or safety or for the protection of others. Thus far, the arrangement was perfectly lawful. It became unlawful if it was used to improvise a long-term community treatment order. This would be done by recalling the patient from leave just before the detention was due to expire, purely in order to renew the detention, so that he or she could then be sent on leave again. In those circumstances it could not be certified, as the Act requires, that the patient could only receive necessary treatment by being detained. McCullough J. held that detention for treatment could only be initiated or renewed if the patient was felt to require

10 Health Circular HC(90)23/LASSL(90)11 (*The Care Programme Approach*). In Wales, there is the All Wales Mental Illness Strategy (See, now, *Guidance on the Care in the Community of People with a Mental Illness* WHC(95)40).
11 This includes HSG(94)27/LASSL(94)4, *Guidance on the Discharge of Mentally Disordered people and their Continuing Care in the Community*; HSG (94)5 on Supervision Registers; the Department of Health Guide, *Building Bridges* (1995) on arrangements for inter-agency working for the care and protection of severely mentally ill people; HSG(96)6\LASSL (96)6 and NHS Executive EL(97)1, op. cit., n. 3. The Mental Health (Patients in the Community) Act 1995 has also been accompanied by a supplement to the Mental Health Act Code of Practice (HSG (96(11)\WHC (96)11), *Guidance on Supervised Discharge and Related Provisions*.
12 Mental Health Act Commission, *First Biennial Report* (1985) para. 8.12.
13 *R.* v. *Hallstrom ex parte W (No. 2)* and *R.* v. *Gardner and another ex parte L* [1986] 2 All E.R. (Q.B.D.) 306.

107

a period of in-patient treatment. Extended leave could be used to enforce community treatment for a limited period only. The patient's detention could not be renewed when he or she was on leave unless he or she required in-patient treatment.[14]

In the debates leading to the 1983 Act the psychiatric profession had been markedly unenthusiastic about proposals for a community treatment order, since the 'long leash' was perfectly effective from their point of view. Recall was by doctor's order in writing and beyond that there were no procedural requirements of consultation. After *Hallstrom* there were repeated proposals for compulsory powers to be granted over mentally disordered patients who are well enough to survive outside hospital provided that they continue to comply with their medication.

The opponents of compulsory community medication say that if someone is well enough not to need detention in hospital, it is an unwarrantable infringement of their individual freedom to require them to accept medication, usually depot antipsychotic drugs, which may have unpleasant and permanently damaging side-effects. There is also the problem that the requirement to continue with medication is difficult to subject to legal review. How can a patient who is well demonstrate that this is because he or she is well rather than because of the drugs he or she is taking? The advocates of community treatment orders say that it is impossible to provide these patients with the continuing care which they need in the community without imposing on them an obligation to accept medication. The medicine is necessary to keep the person from relapsing into the throes of an illness which is progressively more debilitating with each onset, and which if not checked by medicine may lead to the loss of family, friends, job, and home, and even to offending behaviour and imprisonment. On this view, the potential adverse side-effects of the compulsory medication must be weighed against the strong probability of serious deterioration in the patient's condition without it.

In the wake of the Benjamin Silcock case (where a patient receiving community care was videoed jumping into the lion's den at London Zoo) and the killing of Jonathan Zito by Christopher Clunis (a schizophrenia sufferer who been detained many times and whose community care had broken down) the Conservative government introduced supervision registers for patients posing a risk to themselves or others, guidance on risk assessment prior to discharge, and the legal centre-piece of their strategy, the Mental Health (Patients in the Community) Act 1995. Clunis should have been receiving s. 117 aftercare when he killed Jonathan Zito, but he had 'lost touch' with the service. The aim of the 1995 Act was to increase community controls over patients by obliging patients to accept s. 117 aftercare services, and by obliging community supervisors to ensure that the services are delivered.

14 See now, also, *Barker* v. *Barking, Havering and Brentwood Community Healthcare NHS Trust* 30 July 1998 (CA).

The Conservative government rejected a number of other options to ensure compliance with medication in the community. One was to empower nurses to medicate forcibly in patients' own homes. There were great concerns from community psychiatric nurses to avoid being put in the position of forcibly medicating a person in their own home. This would be a twofold invasion of the right of privacy guaranteed by Article 8, an infringement of the 'home as castle' principle, and an invasion of the sanctity of the person. Moreover it is likely to be seen by patients and not a few psychiatric nurses as a violation of the therapeutic relationship leading to the destruction of trust. To be justified under Article 8(2) of the Convention, it would need to be necessary in a democratic society for the protection of health or the prevention of disorder or crime, and would need to be in accordance with law. This would mean that the intrusion would need to be proportionate to the goal being pursued. Another possibility rejected was to provide for the immediate re-detention of a patient who has ceased to take medication, without needing objective evidence that the person is currently mentally disordered of a nature or degree warranting detention. Unless it was an emergency, this would have risked infringement of Article 5(1).

The option chosen was to have a power limited to patients who had been detained and were entitled to s. 117 aftercare services who could be subject to 'supervised discharge'. Such patients were given a supervisor who was responsible for ensuring that they received aftercare services. Patients could be required to live at a specified residence, to attend specified places for medical treatment, education or training, and to grant access to their homes to mental health professionals. If they did not attend the required place for treatment, they could be taken and conveyed there with the use of reasonable force by the supervisor or anyone authorized by the supervisor. According to the Code of Practice they could not be forcibly treated there, unless there was a common law emergency, and could not be detained there, but they could be assessed with a view to compulsory admission.[15]

The psychiatrists who advocated community supervision estimated that there were about 3,000 patients who would benefit from the new power. Initial impressions are that it has been very little used. Although for the first time the applicant for compulsory powers is the psychiatrist rather than a social worker, the power is subject to a maze of form-filling, consultation, and other procedural requirements. Less than three years after the 1995 Act came into force the Labour government has appointed the scoping group, which has been given the task of ensuring, in the words of the Minister, Paul Boateng, that the government's new policy aims were underpinned by 'modern and robust legislation':

15 Following the decision of the House of Lords in *R.* v. *Bournewood Community and Mental Health NHS Trust, ex parte L* (Secretary of State for Health and others intervening) [1998] 3 All E.R. 289, if a patient lacks capacity they may be treated under common law without consent, or even detained pending compulsory admission, if it is in their best interests.

[W]ith our safety plus approach, the law must make it clear that non-compliance with agreed treatment programmes is not an option. We are determined to develop comprehensive mental health services which are safe, sound and supportive. They must protect the public and provide safe and effective care for mentally ill people. New legislation is needed to support our new policies, for example to provide extra powers to treat patients in a range of clinical settings, including, where necessary, in the community, and to ensure a proper balance between the interests of the public and the rights of the individual. Carers too should have rights, as well as responsibilities. Too often they have been left to pick up the pieces, but were never given any rights at the moment of a crisis affecting those for whom they have been responsible.

The group's terms of reference require it to advise on changes needed to support compulsory treatment where deemed necessary for those patients not formally detained, to consider 'interface issues' with other relevant national legislation or proposed legislation (this obviously includes the Human Rights Act, and the possible Incapacity Act proposed by the Law Commission), and to consider the implications of recent case law (including Strasbourg case law) and recommendations made in inquiry reports into homicides by psychiatric patients. They must also take on board the views of service providers and 'users/carers', consider the scope for defining the rights of carers, and advise on how these might be taken into account in preparing new legislation. The remainder of this article looks at current debates about reform of mental health law and the potential impact of Convention rights in developing an ideology of entitlement to adequate hospital and community services.

LAWFUL PSYCHIATRIC DETENTION AND ARTICLE 5(1)(e)

1. The Winterwerp criteria

Article 5(1) lists a number of grounds on which deprivation of liberty is permitted, one of which is Article 5(1)(e), 'unsoundness of mind'. A mentally disordered offender who is convicted of a criminal offence and sent to hospital will be detained on the basis of Article 5(1)(a) as well as 5(1)(e).[16] The path-breaking case in relation to the rights of mentally disordered patients was Winterwerp v. The Netherlands (1979), where the European Court held that in order for a detention on grounds of unsoundness of mind to be lawful, unless it is an emergency, the government has to be able to show by reliable evidence before a competent national authority:

(i)   that a true mental disorder has been established by objective medical expertise;
(ii) that the mental disorder is of a kind or degree warranting compulsory confinement; and

16 X, op. cit., n. 8.

110

(iii)   the validity of continued confinement depends upon the persistence of such a disorder.[17]

The competent authority in England and Wales is the 'hospital manager' (the National Health Service Trust which runs the hospital) for non-offender patients and the criminal court for an offender patient. The objective medical expertise comes from the requirement that a doctor recognized under s. 12 of the Mental Health Act 1983 as having psychiatric expertise and another doctor must furnish medical recommendations certifying that the patient has a mental disorder of the relevant nature or degree and that detention is necessary in the interests of the patient's health or safety or for the protection of others. A counterweight to medical opinion is provided by the fact that the application must come from an approved social worker or the patient's nearest relative.

2.   *True mental disorder*

The patient must be suffering from a true mental disorder. The fact that a person's views or behaviour deviate for the norms prevailing in a particular society will not justify detention.[18] The 1983 Act provides that no-one shall be treated as mentally disordered for the purposes of the Act by reason only of sexual deviancy or dependence on alcohol or drugs. They may be detained if there are some other symptoms of mental disorder. Both the Convention and the 1983 Act require the mental disorder to be of a kind/nature or degree justifying detention. The term nature or degree is disjunctive, and so a person may be detained if their mental disorder is of a nature warranting detention (severe chronic schizophrenia), even if it is not currently of a degree in terms of overt symptoms.[19] Unlike jurisdictions which require dangerousness to self or to others, the English system allows detention in the interests of health or safety or for the protection of others. This is within the margin of discretion permitted to Council of Europe member states.

3.   *Detention on grounds of unsoundness of mind and the right to a therapeutic environment*

The purpose of psychiatric detention is therapeutic, which prompts the question whether the Convention may be deployed to enforce minimum standards

17 *Winterwerp* v. *The Netherlands* (*European Court of Human Rights Judgments and Decisions*, series A, vol. 33 (1979) at para. 39).
18 id., paras. 37–8.
19 *R.* v. *Mental Health Review Tribunal ex parte Smith* Popplewell J. 4 August 1998 CO/430/98. See, also, the Mental Health Act Commission paper, 'The Threshold for Admission and the Relapsing Patient' August 1998. The question of the point at which a patient in the community who has ceased to accept medication may be detained is a key battleground in the debate about community controls.

111

of treatment. The Strasbourg institutions have shown great reluctance to apply the stigma of 'inhuman and degrading' treatment (contrary to Article 3) to conditions in psychiatric units. Treatment will be inhuman only if it reaches a level of gravity involving considerable mental or physical suffering, and degrading if the person has undergone humiliation or debasement involving a minimum level of severity.[20] In making an assessment in a given case, regard must be had to the surrounding circumstances including the particular conditions, the stringency of the measure, its duration, the objective pursued, and its effects on the person concerned.[21]

One of MIND's test cases was *B.* v. *United Kingdom*[22] (1975), where the conditions in Broadmoor special hospital were alleged to amount to a breach of Article 3. The Butler committee on mentally disordered offenders produced an interim report in 1974 and had expressed themselves astonished and shocked at the overcrowding in some of the wards, with patients living out of suitcases, and with beds eighteen inches apart. B. complained that the living conditions in Broadmoor remained overcrowded and insanitary, that there was lack of work and a violent atmosphere, and that this was inhuman or degrading treatment. Five members of the Commission visited Broadmoor. The Commission agreed that the overcrowding on some of the wards was deplorable and found that the facilities in Broadmoor were extremely unsatisfactory, but nevertheless expressed the opinion that they did not amount to a breach of Article 3.[23] The narrow margin of the Commission vote was a significant warning shot for the government, even though the majority view suggested that conditions would need to be very bad indeed for the level of severity required for a breach of Article 3 to be attained.

In *Dhoest* v. *Belgium*[24] the Commission rejected a complaint of inhuman and degrading treatment by a patient who was often strapped to a bed and sedated with tranquillisers. Dhoest also argued that there had been a breach of Article 5(1)(e), because given the fact that he was detained as a person of unsound mind, he was entitled to appropriate treatment in order to ensure that he was not detained longer than absolutely necessary. He submitted that he did not receive any form of therapy and that the only medical treatment he received consisted of drugs. The Commission reaffirmed its view that, in principle, Article 5(1)(e) was concerned with the question of the actual deprivation of liberty of mental health patients and not their treatment.[25]

20 *Commission* v. *Ireland*, judgment of 18 January 1978, series A, vol. 25, paras. 162, 167, and 179–81.
21 Application no. 10448/83, *Sylvain Dhoest* v. *Belgium Report of the Commission* (adopted on 14 May 1987) para. 118.
22 Application no 6870/75, *European Commission of Human Rights Decisions and Reports*, decision on admissability of 14 May 1977, vol. 10, 37.
23 European Commission of Human Rights, *Stock-taking on the European Convention on Human Rights* (1984) 186; *European Commission on Human Rights Decisions and Reports*, report adopted by the Commission 7 October 1981, vol. 32, 5.
24 *Dhoest*, op. cit., n. 21.
25 id., paras. 143–6. See, also, no. 8225/78, *Ashingdane* v. *United Kingdom*, Comm. Report 12 May 1983, para. 78.

However, a most interesting development has come with the Court's 1998 judgement in *Aerts* v. *Belgium*.[26] Here the European Court held that, where the sole basis of detention is unsoundness of mind (Article 5(1)(e)), an anti-therapeutic environment may contravene Article 5(1), even if it is not severe enough to amount to inhuman and degrading treatment. Mr Aerts was arrested on 14 November 1992, after attacking his ex-wife with a hammer. In January 1993 a Belgian court ordered his detention on remand in an institution to be designated by the relevant mental health board and specified that, pending the board's decision, he was to be provisionally held in the psychiatric wing at Lantin Prison. The board designated the Paifve Social Protection Centre as the place where he was to be detained on 22 March 1993, but he was not transferred there until 27 October 1993.

Aerts complained of breaches of, *inter alia*, Article 3 and Article 5(1). The Lantin psychiatric wing had been criticized in 1994 by the European Committee for the Prevention of Torture and Inhuman and Degrading Treatment as unsuitable for the care of people with mental health problems, since there was neither regular medical attention nor a therapeutic environment. Nevertheless the Court followed the line adopted in previous case-law on Article 3, adopting a very strict view of what is required to bring ill-treatment under the umbrella of inhuman and degrading treatment. The Committee for the Prevention of Torture had found the standard of care at Lantin fell below the minimum acceptable from an ethical and humanitarian point of view and that prolonging patients' detention there for lengthy periods carried an undeniable risk of deterioration in their mental health. However, the Court held that there was no proof of deterioration in the applicant's mental health. The living conditions at Lantin did not seem to have had such serious effects on his mental health as would bring them within Article 3. They did not reach the level of severity necessary to amount to inhuman or degrading treatment.

The most interesting feature of the Court's ruling from the point of view of advancing the ideology of entitlement came in relation to Mr Aerts's Article 5(1) complaint regarding his detention in the psychiatric wing of Lantin prison after the March 1993 decision to detain him in Paifve Social Protection Centre. The Court upheld this complaint because the proper relationship between the aim of the detention and the conditions in which it took place had been deficient. As he had not been convicted of any offence, his detention could not be justified under Article 5(1)(a). The only permissible justification left was Article 5(1)(e), detention on grounds of unsoundness of mind. The Court held that there had to be some relationship between the ground of permitted deprivation of liberty relied on and the place and conditions of detention. In principle, the detention of a person as a mental health patient would only be lawful for the purposes of Article 5(1)(e) if effected in a hospital, clinic, or other appropriate institution. In Mr Aerts's

26 Judgment of European Court of Human Rights, 30 July 1998.

113

case the Belgian Mental Health Board had expressed the view that the situation was harmful to him, as he was not receiving the treatment required by the condition giving rise to detention.

Here we have an apparent denial by the Court of the Commission's line in *Dhoest* that Article 5(1)(e) was concerned with the question of the actual deprivation of liberty of mental health patients and not their treatment. Obviously standards and conditions will have to fall very low indeed for the therapeutic purpose to be destroyed. However, it seems now that where the detention is based on Article 5(1)(e) alone, complaints about conditions in the place of detention are better brought under Article 5 than Article 3.

The *Aerts* ruling was not the first indication of the Court's preparedness to attach positive rights to services to Article 5. In October 1997 the Court delivered judgment in *Stanley Johnson* v. *United Kingdom*,[27] a complaint alleging breach of Articles 5(1) and 5(4) (the right to seek review of the lawfulness of detention before a court which must have the power to order discharge). Johnson had been found not to be suffering from mental disorder by a mental health review tribunal, which had given him a conditional discharge, deferred until suitable arrangements could be made for his reception into a hostel. Patients are entitled to seek review of their detention before a tribunal once in every twelve months. Where, in such cases, a tribunal defers conditional discharge until suitable arrangements can be made, and no arrangements are made before the case next comes before a tribunal, the order for conditional discharge lapses. Johnson was found by three tribunals (1989, 1990, 1991) not to be suffering from mental disorder, but on each occasion his conditional discharge was deferred until a suitable hostel could be found, and none ever was. He was finally released following a tribunal hearing in 1993. He complained to the European Commission on Human Rights on the basis that his detention contravened Articles 5(1) and (4) because the unsoundness of mind which formed the necessary basis of his continued detention was no longer present. The Commission found that his complaint raised complex and serious issues which required determination on their merits.

The European Court held that there had been a breach of Article 5(1). The court rejected the argument that a finding by an expert authority that a person is no longer suffering from the form of mental illness which led to his confinement must inevitably lead to his immediate and unconditional release into the community. This would be an unfortunate curtailment of the expert authority's discretion to assess; part of the 'margin of appreciation' left to the national authorities. Nevertheless, discharge must not be unreasonably delayed, and there must be safeguards, including judicial review, to prevent this. The tribunal had to have the powers to ensure that a placement could be secured within a reasonable period of time.

---

27 European Commission on Human Rights Decision on Admissibility, 18 May 1995, 32520/93. Judgment of the European Court of Human Rights, 24 October 1997, *European Court of Human Rights Report of Judgments and Decisions* (1997–VII) no. 55, 2391.

114

Very often MHRTs find patients to be suffering from mental disorder which would not be of a nature or degree warranting detention if only community care provision could be made. Often the reason for non-provision of community care is lack of resources. In *R.* v. *Gloucestershire County Council ex parte Barry*,[28] the House of Lords held that a local authority could take its resources into account in meeting need for community care under s. 2 of the Chronically Sick and Disabled Persons Act 1970, like s. 117, a community care duty. The fact that a person would not require detention given adequate community care support could be used to base an argument based on Article 5. Failure to provide, and failure to fund that care are breaches of Article 5 because they are consigning a person to detention which would not otherwise be necessary. By failing to provide positive rights the patient's negative rights would be infringed.

4. *Detention of incapable patients: the intersection of common law, the 1983 Act, and the Convention*

One of the key issues in mental health practice is whether compliant mentally incapacitated patients who are not detained under the Act should be given the benefit of similar safeguards to those provided for detained patients in relation to their placement or their treatment without consent. The Law Commission proposed a new statutory jurisdiction based on a locally responsive Court of Protection which would make decisions about the care of mentally incapacitated adults, adjudicating on disputes and making decisions in the best interests of patients.[29] Elderly or profoundly learning disabled incapable patients are often admitted informally without using the powers of compulsory admission.

Informal admission was introduced in 1959 to allow for the admission without detention of people who lack capacity to consent to admission, as long as they do not resist or try to leave. The intention was that under the 1959 Act detention was to be used only for those who resist admission. Everyone else would be admitted informally. But informal patients are not entitled to review of their placement in hospital by a mental health review tribunal, nor are they entitled to a second opinion if treated without consent with psychotropic drugs or ECT. Since 1959 incapable non-resisting patients have been admitted informally, only being detained if they resisted. This has given rise to the phenomenon of *de facto* detention, where incapable patients are placed in hospital without being detained but, in their own interests, would be prevented from leaving if they attempted to do so.

The issue of whether it was lawful to admit informally an adult patient who was incapable of consenting to admission was raised in *R.* v. *Bournewood Community and Mental Health NHS Trust, ex parte L*

28 [1997] 2 W.L.R. 459.
29 Law Commission, *Mental Incapacity*, Law Com. no. 231 (1995).

115

(Secretary of State for Health and others intervening).[30] L was a 48-year-old profoundly learning disabled man. After many years as a hospital in-patient, he had been living for some years in the community with a family, the Enderbys, who were paid under an adult fostering scheme to look after him. One day whilst at a day centre, he became disturbed. On this occasion the Enderbys could not be contacted. A local doctor attended and sedated L His care worker arranged for him to be taken to the accident and emergency ward of the local hospital. L was initially calm and relaxed, but while at the Accident and Emergency Unit he became increasingly disturbed, was again given sedation and was admitted 'informally', without using statutory powers of detention, to the mental health behavioural unit at the hospital, under the care of the clinical director for learning disabilities, a consultant psychiatrist. Although incapable of consenting to admission, once in hospital he made no attempt to leave.[31]

The doctor based her decision to admit L informally on the principle that incapacitated patients need not be admitted compulsorily as long as they do not resist. The Enderbys were prevented from visiting him, in case he might become distressed and want to leave the hospital with them. L did not resist admission, nor did he seek to leave. If he had, the doctor would have detained him. By not detaining L under the 1983 Act, the doctor deprived him of the right to review of his detention by a mental health review tribunal. L sought judicial review of the decision to detain him, habeas corpus directed at the Trust, and an action for damages for false imprisonment. To obtain that redress he had to establish (i) that he had been detained or subject to imprisonment and (ii) that the detention was unlawful.

At first instance, Owen J. held that L was not entitled to a remedy because had not been detained as he had been free to leave at all times until his psychiatrist took steps to 'section' him, or some other member of staff attempted to stop him leaving. The Court of Appeal granted his appeal, holding that he was detained because those who had control over the premises had (a) the intention that he should not be permitted to leave those premises, and (b) the ability to prevent him from doing so. The Court of Appeal further held that his detention was unlawful, because informal admission was unlawful if the patient was incapable of consenting to it.

The Court of Appeal ruling overturned the fundamental assumption of the régime of statutory powers, namely, that informal admission could be based on the absence of dissent. The Court of Appeal considered that the active consent of a capable patient was needed before there could be a non-compulsory admission. This would have meant a vast increase in the numbers of patients who were formally detained, and a dramatic increase in the workload

---

30 [1998] 3 All E.R. 289.
31 He had no ability to express consent or dissent to treatment (although he could manifest unhappiness at specific treatment). He was unable to express preference as to residing at one place rather than another.

116

of bodies such as mental health review tribunals and the Mental Health Act Commission.[32] Because of the implications of the ruling, the Department of Health underwrote the Trust's appeal to the House of Lords and also intervened in the case. They emphasized the cost of the Court of Appeal decision in terms of extra professional time involved in assessing for compulsory admission and in providing the external safeguards normally attaching to compulsory admission. An undesirable prospect of cost and diversion of time from clinical care was compellingly outlined in the affidavits.

The House of Lords allowed the appeal unanimously, holding that, whether or not L had been detained, his admission and retention by the Trust was justified at common law on grounds of necessity. They divided 3-2 over the question of whether L was detained. The majority held that the Court of Appeal had erred in finding that L was detained since he had made no attempt to leave and had been accommodated on an unlocked ward. It could not therefore be said that he had actually been deprived of his liberty. Lords Nolan and Steyn considered that L had been detained. Lord Steyn declared that the case fell 'on the wrong side of any reasonable line that can be drawn between what is or what is not imprisonment or detention' and described the suggestion that L was free to go as 'a fairy tale':

> L was detained because the health care professionals intentionally assumed control over him to such a degree as to amount to a complete deprivation of his liberty.[33]

Five of the nine judges who considered L's position at English law considered him to have been detained. Despite the existence of an extensive case law on detention under the European Convention on Human Rights, the speeches in the House of Lords betray no sign of this. Convention points were put on behalf of L, but none were taken up, somewhat surprising given the imminence of 'incorporation.' This would have been an ideal case for their Lordships to take note of Convention rights, even under existing *Brind* principles.[34] They declined to do so.

Would L's treatment amount to a deprivation of liberty under the Convention? In order for Article 5 to be engaged, there must be a 'deprivation of liberty', 'arrest', or 'detention'. 'Deprivation of liberty' has been held to be relative; to call for an examination of the facts of each particular case; and ultimately to be a matter for the European Court of Human Rights. At English law the key questions are whether the alleged detainee is confined within a defined space, and is subject to restraint on freedom of movement.[35]

---

32 For a critical appraisal of the second opinion system, see P. Fennell, *Treatment Without Consent: Law, Psychiatry and the Treatment of Mentally Disordered People since 1845* (1995).
33 [1998] 3 All E.R. 289, at 307.
34 *R. v. Secretary of State for the Home Department ex parte Brind* [1991] A.C. 696.
35 Duke LJ., in *Meering v. Grahame White*, quotes the following definition from the common law authority Termes de la Ley: '"Imprisonment" is no other thing, but the restraint of a man's liberty, whether it bee in the open field or in the stocks or in a cage in the street or in a man's own house, as well as in the common gaole; and in all places the party so restrained is said to be a prisoner so long as he hath not his liberty freely to goe at all times, to all places whither he will . . .'. (1920) 122 *Law Times* 44, at 51.

117

In deciding whether there has been a deprivation of liberty in each case the European Court of Human Rights takes account of a range of factors such as the nature, duration, effects, and manner of execution of the penalty or other measure in question.[36] In *Guzzardi* v. *Italy* the European Court of Human Rights concluded that the confinement of a suspected Mafioso to a small island pending trial, and limiting his contact with others did not amount to a deprivation of liberty as it did not have the requisite 'degree or intensity'. However, in the later case of *Ashingdane*, the Court held the applicant to be a detained patient in the sense that his liberty had been 'circumscribed both in fact and in law' (he had been subject to a hospital order with restrictions under the 1959 Act) even though he had been permitted to leave the hospital on various occasions. He had been kept on a closed ward in a local psychiatric hospital for ten months following transfer from the top security of Broadmoor Special Hospital, before being moved to an open ward. The Court held that he had been detained throughout, even when he was on the open ward.[37] The question in L's case from the European point of view is whether the nature, duration, effects, and manner of execution of his admission and retention were such as to warrant the appellation 'deprivation of liberty'. Did it have the requisite degree and intensity?

The code of practice on the Mental Health Act advises that an incapable person should only be detained if he 'persistently and purposefully' tries to leave hospital. In other words, before there can be a restraint, there must be a countervailing impulse on the part of the patient to leave. Whilst this may be acceptable as a general principle, Mr L's situation differed because he was deprived of association with the Enderbys, and they with him, in case he might become agitated and seek to leave. In a sense advantage was being taken of his incapacity and his limited ability to express his emotions.

I have argued elsewhere that the deprivation of association with the Enderbys, as well as amounting to a potential violation of all their right of family life under Article 8, would probably be treated by the Strasbourg Court as an aggravating factor situation sufficient to make L's admission and retention a deprivation under Article 5.[38] L's liberty was more 'circumscribed in fact' than in *Ashingdane*'s case. The difference between the cases was that L's liberty was not circumscribed in law, because his detention had not been formalized. But because his freedom was not 'circumscribed under law', neither he nor the Enderbys could challenge his retention in hospital through the tribunal system.

The fact that he was deprived of association with the Enderbys goes to the nature and effects of the measure, as well as its degree and intensity. This fact, it is suggested, makes this a deprivation of liberty. It might be that on the facts of this case the European Court would find that there had

36 Engel case judgment of 8 June 1976, paras. 63–64.
37 Ashingdane case judgment of 28 May 1985, para. 42.
38 P. Fennell, 'Doctor Knows Best: Therapeutic Detention Under Common Law, the Mental Health Act and the European Convention' (1998) 6 *Medical Law Rev.* 322–53.

been detention, but that it would not be detention unless there were some aggravating factor such as deprivation of association with relatives or carers, or refusal to let him leave if he persistently and purposely seeks to go. If so, admission of compliant incapacitated patients would probably not have the requisite severity to amount to detention, as long as they were not denied access to loved ones. This would mean that informal admission would be lawful under the Convention for the vast majority of incapacitated patients.

If this is correct, then any incapacitated patient who is being kept in hospital against the wishes of his or her family or carers should be detained, so that there may be some adjudication as to whether the hospitalization is necessary. Looked at in terms of detention, only L's Article 5 rights were infringed, but, viewed in terms of the right of family life, both L's and the Enderbys' rights under Article 8 were infringed.

Article 8 provides that everyone has the right to respect for his or her private and family life, home, and correspondence. In *X. v. Iceland*, the Commission held that 'the right comprises to a certain degree the right to establish and to develop relationships with other human beings, especially in the emotional field for the development and fulfilment of one's own personality'.[39] Any interference by a public authority with this right must be in accordance with the law. Article 8(2) provides that 'there shall be no interference with this right except such as in accordance with the law and is necessary in a democratic society for . . . the protection of health'.

The authorities created a family life for L, placing him through an adult fostering scheme, but then, on clinical grounds, took it away, albeit temporarily. The question is whether the right of family life could be interfered with under common law on the say-so of the doctor and still be 'in accordance with the law'. The phrase 'in accordance with the law' has been held not merely to mean in accordance with domestic law. It has a qualitative component, requiring the law to be 'compatible with the rule of law':

> It implies that there must be a measure of protection in domestic law against arbitrary interferences by public authorities with the rights safeguarded by Article 8(1).[40]

Although 'law' can include judge-made law as well as legislation, the law should be foreseeable in its effects.[41] The fact that it confers discretion on the doctor is not in itself inconsistent with the requirement of foreseeability, subject to the proviso that:

> the scope of the discretion and the manner of its exercise are indicated with sufficient clarity, having regard to the legitimate aim of the measure in question, to give the individual adequate protection against arbitrary interference.[42]

---

39 6825/74 *European Commission of Human Rights Decisions and Reports*, vol. 5, 86–7, decision of 18 May 1976.
40 Malone judgment of 2 August 1984, series A, no. 82, para. 67, p. 32.
41 id., para. 66, p. 31.
42 Gillow judgment of 24 November 1986, series A, no. 109, para. 51, p. 21.

The law, written and unwritten, must indicate with reasonable clarity the scope and manner of exercise of the relevant discretion.[43] The prime reason for this decision was to prevent L from becoming agitated should he want to go home with the Enderbys. But is this a reason to deprive him of access to them and they to him, without right of appeal? Was the prime motivation to avoid L attempting to go with them, hence triggering a need to detain him formally? There are powers to detain under the Act which would have been available in L's case, and to deprive L of association with the Enderbys risks becoming an arbitrary interference if it was done to avoid having to use those powers and to avoid the statutory review procedures.

If there is a 'deprivation of liberty', this must be carried out in accordance with a procedure prescribed by law. The phrase 'in accordance with a procedure prescribed by law' in Article 5(1) has been held to require compliance with procedural and substantive rules of domestic law. Moreover, that domestic law must be in accordance with the Convention and the general principles expressed or implied therein. In *Winterwerp* v. *The Netherlands*, the Court held that:

> The notion underlying the term is one of fair and proper procedure, namely that any measure depriving a person of his liberty should issue from and be executed by an appropriate authority and should not be arbitrary. . . [D]isregard of the domestic law entails breach of the Convention, with the consequence that the Court can and should exercise a certain power of review.[44]

Once there is a detention or a deprivation of liberty, a number of elements are necessary. Article 5 requires a procedure to guarantee elementary fairness. The statutory procedures require this in the form of an application to the hospital managers supported by two medical recommendations. L's psychiatrist could have summoned a social worker to make the application and could have provided one of the medical recommendations herself, on grounds that L was mentally impaired and that his disorder was of a nature or degree warranting admission for assessment in the interests of his own health and his own safety.[45] The safeguards provided are to ensure that the social worker takes a view on whether an application should be made, and that is supported by medical evidence, and that statutory criteria are met. It is doubtful whether any detention on grounds of common law necessity could satisfy the requirements of Article 5, since it would be carried out on the say-so of the consultant psychiatrist, without the need to present objective evidence to any competent authority of the need for detention. Can an individual consultant psychiatrist be an appropriate authority to execute a measure depriving a person of their liberty? How can common law detention 'accord with procedure prescribed by law' if, as the Court said in the passage quoted above, 'disregard of the domestic law entails breach of the Convention'?

---

43 *Kruslin* v. *France* judgment of 24 April 1990, series A, vol. 176-B, para. 79, p. 36.
44 *Winterwerp*, op. cit., n. 17, para. 46.
45 Mental Health Act 1983, s. 2.

120

INTERSECTING LEGAL ORDERS: THE PROBLEM OF COMMON LAW POWERS

In the United Kingdom the matter is further complicated by the existence of common law. Is it disregard of domestic law to proceed under purported common law powers when there is a statutory power available? In *Black* v. *Forsey*[46] Lord Keith eloquently put the case for treating common law powers to detain as no longer existing where legislation had introduced coextensive statutory powers. His Lordship acknowledged that common law confers 'upon a private individual power lawfully to detain, in a situation of necessity, a person of unsound mind who is a danger to himself or others'. However, he went on to say that it was 'impossible to reach any other conclusion than that the powers of detention conferred upon hospital authorities by the scheme were intended to be exhaustive' containing as they did procedures for emergency, short-term and long-term detention. He considered that these powers were:

> [A]bsolutely inconsistent with a possible view that the legislature intended that a hospital authority should have a common law power to detain a patient otherwise than in accordance with the statutory scheme. That scheme contains a number of safeguards designed to protect the liberty of the individual . . . I would therefore hold that any common law power of detention which a hospital authority might otherwise have possessed has been impliedly removed.

Common law powers had to be kept within bounds because their extensive use would undermine the system of statutory safeguards. Lord Griffiths confined the common law power to restrain a lunatic to:

> imposing temporary restraint on a lunatic who has run amok and is a manifest danger either to himself or to others – a state of affairs as obvious to a layman as to a doctor. Such a common law power is confined to the short period of confinement necessary before the lunatic can be handed over to a proper authority.

The general view following *Black* v. *Forsey* was that authorities who had the power to detain under the 1983 Act should use those powers, and the powers are sufficiently broad to permit detention even when the patient is not dangerous. There should be no need to use common law, unless the person needing to impose restraint is not one of those specifically empowered to exercise the extensive powers of detention under the Act. The Court of Appeal in *Bournewood* followed *Black* v. *Forsey*, but in the House of Lords, Lord Goff held that *Black* v. *Forsey*:

> had no relevance to the present case which is concerned with informal admission under the 1983 Act and bringing a patient to hospital to enable him to have the benefit of such admission if he does not object to it.[47]

---

46 1988 S.C. (H.L) 28.
47 [1998] 3 All E.R. 289, at 301.

What happens if relatives and carers object? Under the Mental Health Act, nearest relatives have rights to be consulted over compulsory admission, to seek discharge, and even, as long as it is reasonable, to veto admission for treatment. Admission under common law of a patient who is incapable of protesting, but whose relatives or carers object, undermines the rights of both patient and carers because they are deprived of their statutory rights.

The Mental Health Act contains a range of procedures conferring wide powers on mental health professionals to cover almost any situation where detention and treatment without consent might be necessary.[48] For someone who has these powers to use common law to detain a person without going through the required procedures would appear to be an obvious disregard of domestic law. The Convention does allow detention in cases of emergency without compliance with a procedure prescribed by law. These are the circumstances where the common law has a role to play, to empower a person who has not already the statutory power (for example, a non-specialist nurse), to restrain a patient who might be a danger to self or others from leaving hospital until they can summon a doctor or a specialist nurse who has the statutory powers. Common law should not be an alternative to statutory powers. In order to comply with the Convention, its role should be that of a safety net to cover emergencies where statute has not provided the necessary powers.

The Law Commission recommended allowing people to appoint attorneys to take decisions about their care in the event that they later became incapacitated, and allowing for court appointed care managers to make such decisions if the incapacitated person has not appointed an attorney before becoming incapable. Care managers would be appointed to act in the patient's best interests. Attorneys and care managers would be able to authorise hospitalization for treatment for mental disorder, but not if the person objects. If the incapacitated person objects to admission or treatment, detention under the Mental Health Act would be necessary. However, there is recognition that treatment for mental disorder should be treated separately. If medicines or ECT for mental disorder were to be given to an incapacitated patient admitted informally by a care manager or attorney, a s. 58 second opinion would be required. The Lord Chancellor's Department has recently consulted on a Green Paper entitled *Who Decides? Making Decisions on Behalf of Mentally Incapacitated Adults*.[49] By placing effectively unreviewable

48 Section 2 admission for assessment and treatment for up to 28 days (nearest relative or social worker applies, two medical recommendations needed, one from a doctor with recognized psychiatric experience); section 3 admission for treatment for up to six months renewable (nearest relative or social worker applies, two medical recommendations needed, one from a doctor with recognized psychiatric experience); section 4 emergency admission for assessment for up to 72 hours (nearest relative or social worker applies, only one medical recommendation needed from any doctor; section 5 doctor's (up to 72 hours) and nurse's (up to six hours) holding power for in-patients.

49 Lord Chancellor's Department, *Who Decides? Making Decisions on Behalf of Mentally Incapacitated Adults* (1997).

power in the hands of doctors, the House of Lords in *Bournewood* has given a timely reminder that there is a need for procedures to resolve disputes between carers and professionals about who should have the care of incapacitated people, and about where their best interests lie.

COMPULSORY COMMUNITY POWERS

The Mental Health (Patients in the Community) Act 1995 stops short of empowering mental health professionals to administer treatment forcibly in the community. It also stops short of empowering doctors to admit compulsorily as soon as a patient with a history of detention ceases medication. What it does is to allow patients who have been detained to be subject to supervised discharge, which includes the power to require attendance at a specified place for treatment. If the patient does not attend, s/he may be 'taken and conveyed' but may not be forcibly treated there. The government has now invited the scoping group to find other means of ensuring that non-compliance with agreed treatment programmes is not an option. What limits, if any, are imposed by the Convention?

Amongst the many possible approaches, three seem likely to be considered:

(a) to operate some form of supervised discharge along current lines but with the added possibility that patients could be recalled in the interests of their own health if they stopped medication, and they could remain liable to recall for an extendable and potentially indefinite period;

(b) to require acceptance of treatment (using force if necessary) at the place which the patient is required to attend; or

(c) to require acceptance of treatment, using force if necessary, in the patient's own home.

The only one of these options to which Article 5 would potentially apply is (a). In the case of (b) and (c) the measures would not amount to a 'deprivation of liberty', so Article 5 would not apply.[50]

Article 8(1) of the Convention provides that everyone shall have the right to respect for his or her private and family life, home, and correspondence. In *L* v. *Sweden*,[51] the European Commission on Human Rights held that

---

50 *L* v. *Sweden* application 10801/84 *European Commission of Human Rights Decisions and Reports*, vol. 61, 62–91; Report of the Commission adopted 3 October 1988. See, also, *W* v. *Sweden* application 12778/87, decision of 9 December 1988, *European Commission of Human Rights Decisions and Reports*, vol. 59, 158–61.

51 Application 10801/84, *European Commission of Human Rights Decisions and Reports*, vol. 45, 181–9, decision of 20 January 1986 on admissibility; Report of the Commission adopted 3 October 1988.

123

a decision provisionally to release someone who had been detained in a psychiatric hospital constitutes an interference with his right to respect for private life. However, the Commission went on to declare the application manifestly ill-founded, holding that the measure was justified in the interests of the person's health under Article 8(2) which provides that: 'There shall be no interference with this right except such as is in accordance with the law and is necessary in a democratic society for . . . the protection of health' and the applicant could not be said to have an 'arguable claim' of a violation of Article 8.[52]

The patient in this case had been provisionally discharged by a Discharge Council consisting of five members – a judge, a psychiatrist, a member with special knowledge of social issues, and two other members. The reason for not discharging the applicant permanently was that there were reasons to believe that she would stop taking her medication if permanently discharged, and this would lead to a permanent deterioration in her health. The Commission held that the decision not to discharge the applicant permanently was necessary in a democratic society for the protection of her health. So provisions granting leave from detention on condition that the patient continues to accept medication are not *per se* a violation of Article 8, as long as they comply with Article 8(2).

The other question in *L* v. *Sweden* was whether Article 6 of the Convention might apply in such a case. Article 6(1) provides that in the determination of his civil rights and obligations . . . everyone is entitled to a fair and public hearing within a reasonable time by an independent and impartial tribunal established by law. The Commission decided that:

> proceedings relating to an individual's detention in a psychiatric hospital do not as such concern that individual's 'civil rights and obligations', unless such detention has effects on the individual's right to administer his property or the like.[53]

The Commission concluded that:

> In substance, it could be said that the issue which was examined by the domestic organs was whether the applicant was still in need of certain medical treatment. In the Commission's opinion this examination did not bear upon the applicant's 'civil rights and obligations', and the outcome of the proceedings was not directly or indirectly decisive for any such rights or obligations.[54]

Accordingly, Article 6(1) did not apply to the proceedings before the Discharge Council and the Psychiatric Council. This approach, whilst in keeping with the Court's narrow view of civil rights and obligations, seems unduly restrictive when applied to deny the opportunity of review of a legal obligation to accept neuroleptic medication with serious side effects.

---

52 *L* v. *Sweden*, op. cit., n. 50, pp. 75–6, para. 93.
53 id., para. 86. Here the Commission relied on *Winterwerp*, op. cit., n. 17, para. 73 and the Commission's report in *Van der Leer* v. *The Netherlands*, 14 July 1988, para. 121.
54 id., paras. 87–8.

124

The applicant also complained of violation of Article 13:

> Everyone whose rights and freedoms as set forth in this Convention are violated shall have an effective remedy before a national authority notwithstanding that the violation has been committed by persons acting in an official capacity.

The Commission observed that Article 13 does not require a remedy under domestic law in respect of any alleged violation of the Convention. It only applies if the individual can be said to have an 'arguable claim' of a violation. As the Commission had already rejected the applicant's Article 8 claim as manifestly ill-founded, there was no arguable claim. Moreover Article 13 does not guarantee a remedy whereby a law can be challenged before a domestic organ, and L was effectively challenging the Swedish law.

Thorold notes that a further approach of seeking to challenge the imposition of medicine with unpleasant side effects under Article 3 was rejected in *Grare* v. *France* and concludes that:

> Community controls, where applied to patients assessed as needing follow-up, therefore appear to be treated as insufficiently invasive or serious to engage any of the relevant Articles of the Convention.[55]

Although the case law is from the Commission and is over a decade old, before the advent of wide scale reliance on community controls, the Convention jurisprudence appears to impose no obligation to review community powers. In England all patients who are subject to community controls via guardianship, supervision in the community, conditional discharge or extended leave have the opportunity to apply to a mental health review tribunal for discharge. MHRTs deal primarily with the question of whether a patient should be discharged from detention. For detained patients there is a general discretion to discharge patients (other than offenders with Home Office restrictions on discharge). But if she or he is to establish *entitlement* to discharge, the burden is on the patient to satisfy the MHRT that the conditions of detention are not met. MHRTs currently come under an obligation to discharge from detention if the patient can satisfy them (a) that he or she is no longer suffering from mental disorder of a nature or degree warranting detention *or* (b) that detention is no longer necessary in the interests of his or her own health or safety or for the protection of others.

The current criteria for discharge mean that a tribunal may refuse discharge as long as it is *not satisfied* that the patient is *not suffering* from mental disorder of a nature or degree warranting detention (the infamous 'double negative'). In relation to community powers, the burden of proof was similarly placed. The Strasbourg institutions have yet to pronounce on the issue. At the admissibility stage in *James Kay* v. *United Kingdom*, one of the applicant's contentions before the Commission was that the tribunal cannot provide an effective remedy 'because it does not have to find positive

---

55 Thorold, op. cit., n. 1, p. 632.

125

evidence that the patient is suffering from mental disorder' but this point was not argued further.[56] As Thorold puts it:

> United Kingdom law allows any such doubts to be resolved against the patient, and in favour of continuing detention. In so doing it is quite possible that the criteria for discharge given to tribunals constitute a violation of Article 5. To ensure compliance the criteria would have to be recast to impose a duty to discharge unless a mental disorder of the requisite severity is found to subsist.[57]

With community powers, the case for reversal of the burden of proof is even more compelling, even though it is not required by the Convention. The patient currently has to show that the absence of symptoms is due to the absence of illness rather than medication, rather than it being for the psychiatrist to satisfy the tribunal that the medicine is needed.

As for the 'ideology of entitlement' to community services, the *Stanley Johnson* case represents the high water mark of Convention case law. Under English law social services and health authorities have duties under s. 117 of the 1983 Act and social services have a duty to assess under s. 47 of the National Health Service and Community Care Act 1990. The case of *Clunis v. Camden and Islington Health Authority*[58] has dealt a set-back to the ideology of entitlement. Here the Court of Appeal held that Clunis could not obtain damages for breach of the duty to provide community care services under s. 117. He was claiming that as a result of the authority's failure to supervise him properly and ensure that he received services, he became ill and killed Jonathan Zito. The Court of Appeal held that he was barred because of the maxim *ex turpi causa non oritur actio*. His plea of diminished responsibility for the homicide accepted that his responsibility was substantially impaired, but did not remove liability for his criminal act. He must be taken to have known what he was doing and that it was wrong (that is, he was not *McNaghten* insane). He could not profit from his own crime. Moreover, the Court held that the wording of s. 117 was not apposite to create a private law cause of action for failure to carry out the duties under the section. Nor would it be fair, just, and reasonable to impose a common law duty of care on the authority.

CONCLUSION

Although it would be rash to say that incorporation will lead to a spate of successful challenges of English mental health law and practice, there are many areas which are open to challenge under the Convention. Currently, the mental health review tribunals are bracing themselves for the implementation of the Act in relation to the delays between application for

56 *James Kay* v. *United Kingdom* application no. 17821/91, admissibility decision 7 July 1993.
57 Thorold, op. cit., n. 1, p. 629.
58 [1998] 3 All E.R. 180.

126

discharge and hearing. In an effort to bring these below eight weeks, to comply with the requirement of speedy review in Article 5(4), some tribunals are sitting without clerks. Without extra resources in terms of clerks and members, there is a danger that the quality of decision-making may deteriorate as members have to focus on administrative aspects of the hearing rather than wholly on their judicial function.

There are glimmerings of a developing jurisprudence whereby rights to a (very) basic level of service are being attached to Article 5. There would appear to be little Convention obstacle to 'the third way' in community treatment; the key question in relation to community powers is how the jurisprudence could develop under Article 8, if the possibility of jurisprudence has not been eliminated by *L* v. *Sweden*. There could be forms of community compulsion, such as forcible medication at home, which are disproportionate in relation to the goal pursued. In *Herczegfalvy* v. *Austria*, the court held that Article 8 had not been infringed because the applicant had not demonstrated that he had the capacity to make treatment decisions. Might this be the beginning of a move towards using decision-making incapacity as well as necessity on health or public order grounds as the gatekeeper concept in relation to community treatment?

Without doubt, the Convention has served detained psychiatric patients well. It remains to be seen whether it will serve those who are subject to community controls, but the signs are inauspicious. Whatever happens, post-'incorporation' we are unlikely to see a case such as *Bournewood*, where an issue of detention, squarely in the scope of Article 5, could be adjudicated by the House of Lords without a single mention of the Convention in the speeches.

JOIN...
THE LAW AND SOCIETY ASSOCIATION
AND RECEIVE
LAW & SOCIETY REVIEW
A LEADING JOURNAL FOR THEORY
AND RESEARCH IN STUDIES OF LAW AND SOCIETY

Membership in the Association includes a subscription to *Law & Society Review*. The *Review* has published the highest quality interdisciplinary empirical research and theory for over twenty-five years and has one of the largest circulations in the fields of sociolegal studies. It is a broadly interdisciplinary peer-reviewed journal offering articles on important developments in theory and empirical research on law, legal institutions, and law-related aspects of society. International in scope, the *Review* publishes the work of authors from many countries about their own and other societies and cultures. *Law & Society Review* also offers review essays on current theory, research and comments on the field and its method of inquiry.

Members of the Law and Society Association bring training in law, sociology, political science, psychology, anthropology, economics, history, and other related areas to better understand functioning legal systems in their social and historical context. The **Annual Meeting** of the Association, held in late spring, brings scholars together from around the world. The Association *Newsletter* is also included in membership. Return this application with your dues, and visit our website, www.lawandsociety.org, for further information about the Association, the Annual Meeting, and other programs.

LAW AND SOCIETY ASSOCIATION
Hampshire House-Box 33615
University of Massachusetts
Amherst, MA 01003-3615 USA
Phone: 413 545 4617 / Fax: 413 545 1640 / Email: lsa@legal.umass.edu

MEMBERSHIP APPLICATION
(Please Print)

NAME: _____

ADDRESS:_____

_____

_____

     City   State or Country   Zip

INSTITUTIONAL
AFFILIATION:_____

MEMBERSHIP CATEGORY: Dues are annual by (calendar year). Regular dues are **by income on a sliding scale** (nonU.S. residents calculate what their income would be in USD to determine rate). Dues for 1999 (includes Review Vol. 33):

Regular: Under $15,000 ___ ($30)   **$30,001-$60,000** ___ ($ 70)
       $15,001-$30,000 ___ ($50)   **$60,001-$80,000** ___ ($ 90)
Student ($25)___   **Above $80,000** ___ ($110)

PAYMENT: Check____ or **VISA**____ **MasterCard**____ **Exp. Date**_____

Card #_____

Signature_____

Printed and bound by CPI Group (UK) Ltd, Croydon, CR0 4YY

09/06/2025

14686132-0003